THE LIVING ROOM SERIES

NO OTHER GODS

THE UNRIVALED PURSUIT OF CHRIST

REVISED & EXPANDED

KELLY MINTER

LifeWay Press® Nashville, Tennessee

Published by LifeWay Press® • ©2017 Kelly Minter

Reprinted September 2018

No part of this book may be reproduced or transmitted in any form or by any means, electronic or mechanical, including photocopying and recording, or by any information storage or retrieval system, except as may be expressly permitted in writing by the publisher. Requests for permission should be addressed in writing to LifeWay Press®; One LifeWay Plaza; Nashville, TN 37234-0152.

ISBN 978-1-4300-3235-9
Item 005644897
Dewey decimal classification: 231.7
Subject heading: BIBLE--STUDY \ GOD \ CHRISTIAN LIFE

To order additional copies of this resource, write LifeWay Church Resources Customer Service; One LifeWay Plaza; Nashville, TN 37234-0113; FAX order to 615.251.5933; call toll-free 800.458.2772; email orderentry@lifeway.com; order online at www.lifeway.com; or visit the LifeWay Christian Store serving you.

Printed in the United States of America

Adult Ministry Publishing, LifeWay Church Resources, One LifeWay Plaza, Nashville, TN 37234-0152

Author's literary agent is D.C. Jacobson & Associates LLC, an Author Management Company, www.dcjacobson.com.

TABLE OF CONTENTS

Join Kelly at

 cultivate

A Women's Gathering Around the Word

AT A CULTIVATE EVENT, YOU'LL EXPERIENCE:

 BIBLICAL TEACHING

ACOUSTIC WORSHIP

PRAYER

 A HEART FOR MISSIONS

Dates and locations available at
cultivatevent.com

MEET THE AUTHOR

Kelly Minter is a Bible teacher, author, and singer/songwriter with a desire to serve women of all ages. She has found deep hope and healing through the Bible's truths, making her message personal and relational. Along with her love of Scripture, at the core of her ministry is a deep affection for worship, prayer, and missions, which she blends together at her women's event called Cultivate: A Women's Gathering Around the Word. You can hear her at this biblically based and stylistically inviting event for women of all ages.

Kelly's in-depth Bible studies include: *Ruth: Loss, Love & Legacy*, a study that follows the redemptive story of Ruth, displaying God's providence and purpose even in the most trying circumstances; *Nehemiah: A Heart That Can Break*, an unforgettable journey into the missional heart of God; *What Love Is: The Letters of 1, 2, 3 John*, a study on the love of Christ through the pen of the beloved disciple; and *All Things New: A Study on 2 Corinthians*, our call as believers to shine brightly and distinctly in our current culture. Kelly's music includes *Hymns & Hallelujahs*, which accompanies her *All Things New* Bible study.

Kelly's first memoir, *Wherever the River Runs: How a Forgotten People Renewed My Hope in the Gospel*, is about her life-changing journeys to the Amazon jungle with Justice & Mercy International. Kelly partners closely with JMI, an organization that cares for the vulnerable and forgotten in the Amazon and Moldova. To view more about Kelly's studies, books, music, and Cultivate events, visit www.kellyminter.com.

INTRODUCTION

This Bible study about modern-day idolatry began on a Wednesday night. I couldn't tell you what I wore or what passage of Scripture we studied. You see, this took place before the advent of social media. In other words, before every detail would have been photographed and documented, even down to the flower vases. I invited four of my girlfriends, Lauri, Alli, Anadara, and Carrie, to a Bible study I had yet to write, on a topic still to be determined. Oh, and I had no real experience in writing or teaching Bible studies either—turns out you have to start somewhere.

Making up for the lack of general appeal I decided to offer dinner as part of the package. However, it didn't occur to me until about ten minutes before everyone arrived, and after my dish towel caught fire, that I actually didn't know how to cook. Looking back, it seems a miracle that this study made it past the welcome mat of my condo much less into a rewritten edition a decade later. See? We really do have an all-powerful God.

As I write this new version of *No Other Gods*, I'm both deeply grateful and sobered. Grateful because the Lord did not spare me His severe mercy in dismantling the idols for whom I was living at the time. Sobered because if left to my own desires and rationale I would have missed the unsurpassed blessings I've experienced on the other side of that deconstruction.

I would have missed nearly a decade of dynamic mission trips down the Amazon River on a boat named *The Discovery*. I would have missed the rich community I now have, my church, and the privilege of working with orphans in Moldova. Peace would have been distinctly absent from my life. I wouldn't have been spiritually healthy enough to sustain my dearest friendships or been as present as I needed to be for the six nieces and nephews who call me Aunt. (Actually, they just call me Kelly. I'm trying to be cool and let this go.) And I would have missed an unencumbered walk with Jesus, the peak of all blessings. Simply put, on the other side of my strongholds and ruthless attachments lay surprises I couldn't have imagined that night in my living room with those four girls.

While the blessings of an unrivaled pursuit of Christ run deep for each of us, confronting our modern-day idols is tricky business—false gods just don't stand out like they used to. It's easy to identify a looming statue that a pagan king exalted as an idol in Old Testament times—a man-made golden calf is clearly not the one true God, at least in hindsight. We muse *Why did the ancients ever fall for such things?*

I've discovered that in all our modern-day sophistication, our idols may look different, but our enslavement to them is the same. For many of us, our false gods look more like smartphones than statues. Our idols show up in clothing catalogues and home blogs. They lunge into our in-boxes with "must haves" and "don't miss outs," promising to satisfy our longings. Even when we're simply catching up on our social media feeds, we're suddenly aware of what we don't have but really, really want. We end up saddled with jealousy and feelings of being left out, not realizing those reactions are rooted in the gods we think we need for life and happiness.

Even if you've somehow managed to circumvent technology, you may not be as home free as you think. False gods can masquerade as material possessions, entertainment, food, academic pursuits, investment portfolios, bosses, spouses or friends, or even our ministries. Identifying them, let alone contending with them, can be challenging stuff.

Because I know that freedom is possible and the unrivaled pursuit of Jesus Christ worth it, I've returned ten years later to bring this study to you anew. What you hold in your hands is my life message. I've looked to myriad pleasures to satisfy the ache in my soul, hoping I'd find fulfillment and meaning. I've bought the lie that if I could just have this person or that measure of success, life would finally be all I'd hoped it would be. But nothing has brought me the joy, freedom, and happiness that Christ has given me. No person has plumbed the depths of my heart or revealed its truest desires like He has.

While on the brink of a decision of faith, a friend of mine once said, "In fifteen years I don't want to look back and wonder what God would have done; I want to look back and say, 'Look what He did.'" The idols of our day are tired, predictable, but there's no telling what Jesus will do with a life wholly spent in pursuit of Him. No god can compare to Jesus. He is Lord of all, the great King and Redeemer, Creator and Savior. There is simply no one like Him.

INTRODUCTION

GROUP DISCUSSION

What one thing from this video teaching really resonated with you? Why?

What do you hope to gain from this study and the time spent together?

How would you define a modern-day idol?

As we begin this study, are you already aware of possible false gods in your life? If you're comfortable sharing with the group, explain.

How have you found yourself trying to serve God and your idols? What tensions have you discovered?

What is hindering you from letting go of your false gods?

Video sessions available for purchase or rent at **LIFEWAY.COM/NOOTHERGODS**

PERSONAL GODS

I recently watched my six-year-old nephew, Will, and my five-year-old niece, Harper, play back-to-back soccer games on a Saturday afternoon. Who needs nationally televised college football games when you can catch Team Snickers take on Team Skittles? Right. Watching a kids' soccer game is a fascinating pastime—it's the only sporting event in the world where the ball is in charge. Wherever it goes, so go a swarm of children. At that age, there's little strategy and no spacing of the players across the field. It's basically sixty minutes of babysitting with exercise thrown in.

Will and Harper were especially cute in their cleats, shin guards, shiny shorts, and jerseys. There's something endearing about a child in sporting apparel, holding an enormous bottle of Gatorade®, having no idea what the point of the game is. The lack of soccer acumen was evident when my brother David knelt down, looked Harper dead in the eye, and gave her this coaching tip: "When someone from the other team has the ball, you're allowed to run up and steal it!"

"Dad," Harper said while pointing at his shoulder, "You have a bug on your shirt."

It's easy to sit on the sideline in my camping chair and chuckle at these little ones playing so hard at a game they don't really understand. But the lesson wasn't lost on me. Too many times I've worn all the right Christian gear, run from one end of ministry to the other, watched the latest piece of theology being kicked back and forth over social media, and still totally missed the goal. I've tired myself to the bone on good Christian activities, forgetting why I'd engaged in those activities in the first place.

Jesus addressed the church of Ephesus in the Book of Revelation (Rev. 2:1-7). He praised them for their labor, their endurance of hardship for His name, their strong stance against evil people, and their resilience in not growing weary through trials. In other words, they were looking pretty good in their Christian uniforms. They had sprinted all over the field, even coming through with some defensive slide tackles against the evildoers. But Jesus had this one thing against them: They had forsaken their first love. They'd abandoned Him as the treasure of their hearts. They'd forgotten the whole point of their faith.

> It will all be for your love of Jesus. He is why we're here.

If I have one prayer for you over the next eight weeks it's that as you confront the modern-day idols of your heart you'll reclaim your first love for Jesus. Yes, you'll grow in Bible knowledge, strengthen your faith, gain insight into the reasons you're attached to certain false gods, but it will all be for your love for Jesus. You'll surrender certain idols to Him and lay other ones down, and you'll peer into the blessings that come from a life of obedience. But none of this will matter if along the way you lose sight of Jesus, the One for whom you're doing all this hard work. He is why we're here. I pray each page of this study ultimately points to Him.

Get ready for this journey to be personal. Dealing with your false gods isn't something you can do from an emotionally distant place. Idolatry is too bound up in our hearts for us to fight it with self-righteous intellectualism or pat Sunday School answers. We're going to have to get real about the true treasures of our hearts, share openly with safe and trusted believers, and pray with and for each other. We must step out in faith, say goodbye to some idols that have ruled us for entirely too long, and embrace what the Lord promises to bring in their stead.

When God led me through an intense season of dethroning the idols of my heart, it was the hardest and sweetest time of my life. Hard, because of what I had to let go of. Sweet, because I began to reclaim my first love for Jesus. More than a decade later, I can testify to you that no pursuit in my life has been worth more than the unrivaled pursuit of Christ. It's why I had to come back and present this study to you anew. I don't want you to miss Him for anything in the world.

DAY ONE

DEFINING OUR TERMS

EXODUS 20:3: You shall have no other gods before me (NIV).

As I approach this topic ten years after first writing about what it means to know and serve the one true God, I do so bearing more experience. When God awakened me to the reality of modern-day idolatry all those years ago, all I could see at the time was the choice set before me: continue to fall at the feet of the false gods I was living for or renounce them for the promise of living more fully for Jesus Christ.

Mind you, the choice was clear but not simple. It was fraught with moments of confusion and complex ramifications. Yes, I knew what I needed to do, but leaving behind the comforts of what was familiar and satisfyingly unsatisfying was terrifying. And following Jesus down a path of obedience that felt so narrow there was little room for extras seemed a lonely proposition.

At the time, I knew what obedience meant, but I didn't know what it would yield. The first writing of *No Other Gods* was about identifying and walking away from the idols that hold us captive so that we can make room for God. This revision maintains that theme but also sheds light on what's on the other side—the unrivaled fullness and blessing that accompanies Christ being the absolute Lord of our lives.

We'll discover the adventure and fulfillment of having an intimate relationship with Jesus Christ.

We'll learn what committing to the narrow path of obedience looks like—and how to stay there—so that when the path breaks into wide-open glades of blessing and beauty we're around to experience it. We'll do the hard work of cutting ourselves loose from our modern-day obsessions so we can abide in the Vine, bearing abundant fruit that will matter into eternity. We'll discover the adventure and fulfillment of having an intimate relationship with Jesus Christ that absolutely nothing on earth can begin to compete with.

As you begin this personal journey, know that we'll spend much of our time studying the Israelites at different points in their history since they were quite experienced with false gods of all kinds. Metal or wooden, large or small, religious enough to sit in a sanctuary, homey enough to fit in a living room, a golden cow here, a planet there—if a false god was to be had the Israelites found it or forged it. I wish I could say we don't have the same tendencies today, but the truth is, we do—in spades. Our objects of worship just look a little different.

Besides the Israelites having a history with idols there's another reason they'll fill the bulk of our study.

"Don't become idolaters as some of them were."
1 Corinthians 10:7a

BEGIN TODAY'S STUDY BY READING 1 CORINTHIANS 10:1-13.

List the reasons Paul says "these things" took place, according to verses 6 and 11?

Do not be idolaters, do not indulge in sexual immorality, don't put Christ to the test, do not grumble.

What specific instruction is given at the top of verse 7?

Do not be idolaters.

I don't know if you have a background similar to mine, but I grew up in the church. I was in and out of gatherings like youth group, worship services, and prayer meetings my whole life. I even went to a Christian school. Words like *idols*, *false gods*, and *graven images* were well-known to me. While I'm deeply grateful for what I learned in those settings, overexposure to certain words and phrases can sometimes be detrimental. Over time, these familiar concepts can lose their meaning either through repetition or because they become too connected with things like legalistic teachers or some really odd people.

Terms like *false gods* or *idols* may fall into this category of overfamiliarity for you. Or maybe the opposite is true—you've scarcely been exposed to those words, so instead of sounding churchy and rote, they may sound off-putting and strange. Either way, my hope is that we'll find fresh meaning for old words and possibly new words for old meanings.

Considering our varied backgrounds and the possible connotations that go along with certain words like *false gods*, let's begin by defining our terms. Ponder this definition by Ken Sande:

> Most of us think of an idol as a statue of wood, stone, or metal worshiped by pagan people. … In biblical terms, it is something other than God that we *set our heart on* (Luke 12:29; 1 Cor. 10:19), that motivates us (1 Cor. 4:5), that masters and rules us (Ps. 119:133; Eph. 5:5), or that we trust, fear, or serve (Isa. 42:17; Matt 6:24; Luke 12:4-5). … An idol can also be referred to as a "false god" or a "functional god." [1]

PERSONAL REFLECTION: What new thoughts does this definition bring to your understanding of a false god or idol?

That it can literally be anything that diverts our focus from the Lord — even non-visible things.

When I consider what I set my heart on, what motivates me in life, what controls me, and what I serve with my energy and resources, suddenly I am far from graven images and toe-to-toe with my lust for attention, my attachment to comfort, and my demand for people to meet my needs. These are just hints of what I often look to as my personal saviors.

Look back at the definition and notice the term *functional god*. I especially like the use of this phrase because sometimes it's easier to identify a false god when we see it as something that's functioning for us on a regular basis. Also, I particularly appreciate it because it puts an Old Testament concept in a current light. More on this to come.

PERSONAL TAKE: Explain the difference between a professed god and a functional god.

We can say we believe God, but do our actions line up w/ that?

I put it this way: A professed god is who or what we say is our god; a functional god is who or what actually operates as our god.

In the margin, list some examples of functional gods in our society.

- *Money*
- *Attention*
- *Relationships*
- *Work + success*

Take a look at another definition, this one from Richard Keyes:

> An idol is something within creation that is inflated to function as God. All sorts of things are potential idols, depending only on our attitudes and actions toward them … Idolatry may not involve explicit denials of God's existence or character. It may well come in the form of an over-attachment to something that is, in itself, perfectly good … An idol can be a physical object, a property, a person, an activity, a role, an institution, a hope, an image, an idea, a pleasure, a hero—anything that can substitute for God.[2]

Keyes's definition is profound because he goes beyond merely focusing on our affinities for what is patently sinful. He insightfully points out that it's possible to make gods out of people or things that are in themselves "perfectly good."

John Calvin builds on this concept in another way, "The evil in our desire typically does not lie in what we want, but that we want it too much."[3]

I just got uncomfortable—anyone else? While I've certainly desired what is blatantly wrong, Calvin's definition is more characteristic of my struggles with false gods.

PERSONAL REFLECTION: Write about something in your life that is good in and of itself but has become detrimental simply because you desire it too much.

Getting my education & career started — but then also wanting other people to see me as intelligent & more established than them.

Now that we've defined our terms, we'll look at the first time God addressed idolatry in the Old Testament.

READ EXODUS 20:1-6.

What is the first command given in these verses?

"You Shall have NO OTHER GODS before Me"

PERSONAL REFLECTION: Why is it significant that this is the first of the Ten Commandments? In other words, how do the other nine commandments rest upon this one?

If were not fully devoted to the Lord, we will find ourselves feeling unfulfilled, and chasing after other things, falling into sin, etc.

I think the other nine commandments are irrelevant to us if we neglect the first one. If God is not the God of our lives, the rest of His commandments become mere suggestions. If your exposure to the Ten Commandments began with verse 3, like mine did, you've missed the beautiful introduction found in verses 1-2. The rest of our study will flow from these truths.

SLOWLY READ VERSES 1-2 AND DESCRIBE THE FOLLOWING:

Who does God say He is to the Israelites?

He is their LORD.

What does He say He's done for them?

He brought them up out of Egypt.

But I can't boast bc it's only by the LORD I have accomplished these things.

PERSONAL REFLECTION: How do God's personal relationship with the Israelites and His rescue of them enlighten your perspective on why the first commandment is not to have any gods before God?

He is our father and provider —
God wants us to know He will
keep us safe; nothing else can.
Remember His deeds.

If I've learned anything about false gods over the years it's that they're incapable of satisfying our deepest longings while mercilessly holding us captive. Let me put it to you straight, your idols don't like you. On the other hand, in Exodus 20:2, God declared His deep relationship with His people while also recounting His rescue of them. This personal, pursuing, and liberating love of God will be the power by which we'll demolish the idols of our hearts as we move forward. Nothing but His love will be strong enough for the task ahead.

Nothing else has
our best interest in
mind besides
GOD!

Nothing but His love
will be strong enough
for the task ahead.

9-6-19

DAY TWO

IDENTIFYING
OUR IDOLS

2 KINGS 17:41a: They feared the LORD but also served their idols.

Yesterday we discussed the nature of false gods in modern terminology. Hopefully you already have a better idea of how you've been substituting certain functional gods for God in your life, even allowing them to entangle you. Perhaps you're aware of how you've exalted something to a position it was never meant to hold. It may be a person, career, dream, pleasure, or obsession.

PERSONAL REFLECTION: We're still early in our study, but what false gods can you identify in your life so far?

* money
* creating "my" timeline
* relationship / Husband-to-be

Before I began writing this study the first time around, I struggled to make sense of why general misery had set in like an unhurried front in my life. Why did anxiety feel more the norm than peace? Where was the power of the Christian life I'd learned so much about while growing up in a Christian home? Why were my relationships so tumultuous? I was supposed to have contentment, but within me churned a perpetual desire for what I couldn't possess. I liked the idea of Christ being my satisfaction, but the promise of worldly success and a satisfying human relationship seemed a much more convincing ticket to happiness. I absolutely knew Christ as my Savior, was involved in my church, and remained a fairly knowledgeable Bible student. Why wasn't my life working?

yes!

I briefly shared about this part of my testimony in the opening video along with a passage of Scripture from 2 Kings 17 that yielded the beginning of my answer. I was reading through 2 Kings as part of a one-year Bible plan. These kinds of reading plans can be helpful, because, let's just be honest, when trying to fix your life no one thinks, *let's head to 2 Kings.* Yet as God would have it, this study would grow out of that passage.

In 2 Kings 17, we find the Israelites many years removed from the command God had given them to not have any gods before Him (Ex. 20:3). For years and years the Israelites had yanked on the rope of God's patience and compassion until He finally let His end go. And the rope flew. As a result of their rebellion, the King of Assyria besieged the Israelites who were living in Samaria and deported them to pagan cities under his control. He then took his people from their cities and settled them in Samaria. It was a double exile, if you will: God's chosen people deported to pagan cities, Assyria's pagan people deported to God's city.

READ 2 KINGS 17:6-17. *Look for references to idolatry.*

List the many reasons this tragedy happened, according to this passage. You'll notice the depth of Israel's idolatry as you list each one.

- Sinned against God
- feared other gods
- walked in the customs of the nations
- did things secretly against God
- built high places /pillars
- served idols

- despised God's statutes
- abandoned the Commandments
- made metal images
- worshipped Baal
- burned sons/ daughters

READ VERSES 12-13 AGAIN.

How do we know this punishment hadn't come out of nowhere and could have been avoided?

⤷ God used UNDERLINE EVERY prophet and seer to communicate his warning!

PERSONAL REFLECTION: From your list of reasons why the tragedy occurred, what image or specific form of idolatry reminds you of an idolatrous temptation that the church is currently facing? Explain.

Temptation to put on a "show", stray from spirit-led worship, fame among ppl in church/cliques.

This next part of Scripture about the Assyrians resettling in Israel's Samaria changed my life.

READ 2 KINGS 17:24-41.

Complete each pairing from its corresponding verse:

❏ *Verse 32: They feared/worshiped the LORD, but they …* ~~but also served their own gods.~~
sacrificed in shrines

❏ *Verse 33: They feared/worshiped the LORD, but they …*

Served their own gods.

❏ *Verse 41: They feared/worshiped the LORD, but they …*

also served their carved images.

> They worshiped the LORD, but they also served their own gods.
> 2 Kings 17:33, NIV

Verse 33 deeply convicted me all those years ago. "They worshiped the LORD, but they also served their own gods" (NIV). Verse 41 further compounds the description, "Even while these people were worshiping the LORD, they were serving their idols" (NIV). The people were living split lives, attempting to worship both God and gods. Worshiping the One, while serving the others.

Both verses speak of worship to God but service to idols. For much of my life I worshiped God: singing hymns, reading my Bible, and confessing my belief in Him. Yet, if you could have witnessed what controlled me and what consumed my time, you would have seen that, in many cases, it was my idols. Not carved images but people, career paths, materialism, acceptance, and more. God (on some level) was getting my worship, but my gods were getting my service.

Of course this doesn't really work, as evidenced by verse 34. This dual worship lulls us into thinking that we've still got God on the line because we love Jesus and all. However, in reality our hearts, service, time, trust, and resources are being brought to the feet of something or someone else. Could it be that we're serving our own gods, though we sit on the front row at church and serve coffee in the fellowship hall and lead the mission trips? Do we claim the Bible as our source of truth while our most trusted advisors come from movie screens and social media feeds? Perhaps so many of our struggles—lack of freedom, loss of spiritual desire, slavery to image, perfectionism, confusion, insatiable lusts—have much to do with our futile attempt to serve both God and gods.

PERSONAL REFLECTION: In what areas do you find yourself pulled between worshiping God and serving false gods?

WE'LL END WITH GOD'S PERSONAL PLEA TO HIS PEOPLE BY READING 2 KINGS 17:35-36 AGAIN.

In reference to the false gods of the surrounding nations, the Lord said, "Do not …" and then gave four prohibited actions. What were they?

mind, body,

1. you shall not FEAR other gods.

2. you shall not BOW to other gods.

3. you shall not SERVE them.

4. you shall not SACRIFICE to them.

PERSONAL TAKE: How does each of these actions progressively build on the one before?

moves from a mental idea, to a physical behavior, to a lifestyle.

One of my greatest struggles with idolatry has been putting people in the place of God. Placing those on a pedestal who we think will make life work for us (worship) can lead to a dysfunctional deferring to them in a way only reserved for God (bowing down). This may then lead to our energy being spent on those we've idolized (service), and ultimately to us giving away the dearest parts of ourselves, whether it be our hearts, resources, time, or bodies (sacrifice).

PERSONAL RESPONSE: How do you see this progression unfolding in your struggle with a particular false god? What steps can you take to reverse it?

The more open I am to allowing other gods take my time/resources, the easier it is to compromise & go against your own beliefs.

I believe this divided living is one of the reasons so many of us are stuck. Basically, we've pushed God to the edges. We claim Him as our Savior but we've spared Him little room in our hearts. Our most treasured spaces are occupied by our false gods, and we wonder why God isn't showing Himself strong on our behalf.

This isn't the way it has to be. This wasn't the way it had to be for the Israelites. There's a superior way, and it comes straight from the Lord's mouth. Ponder these words as we close our study together. "Instead, fear the LORD, who brought you up from the land of Egypt with great power and an outstretched arm. You are to bow down to him, and you are to sacrifice to him" (2 Kings 17:36).

I give little sacrifice to God church 1/wk serving 1/mo, bible reading 20m/day. NOT ENOUGH.

PERSONAL RESPONSE: In the space provided, detail the ways you can worship the Lord in each of the corresponding areas.

AREA	WAYS TO WORSHIP
Worship/Fearing	
Bow in worship	
Serving	
Sacrificing	

I know firsthand how difficult and costly this work can be, but nothing will prove more rewarding. As I reflect over the past decade, I do not regret one moment of battle. The one true God set me free from idols that, to this day, I'm no longer a slave of. Absolutely nothing on earth is worth forsaking the life for which the Lord has set you free. I'm cheering you on as you do the work over these next seven weeks together. I promise it's worth everything you've got.

Absolutely nothing on earth is worth forsaking the life for which the Lord has set you free.

DAY THREE
WHAT HOLDS POWER OVER YOU?

EXODUS 2:25: So God looked on the Israelites and was concerned about them (NIV).

As I reflect on this week's topic, I well remember the paralyzing feeling of being under the power of someone or something at different times in my life. Lack of inward freedom is one of the most agonizing experiences of human existence, one I was well acquainted with for an interminable season. However, through the many bouts of weakness and powerlessness, I came to discover the delivering presence of Jesus. He has brought me the freedom that seemed totally unimaginable at the time. It's the same freedom He wants to bring you.

According to the definitions from Day One, what is a false god? Write the answer in your own words. Glance back if necessary.

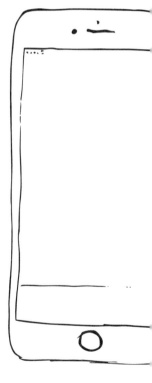

Yesterday I shared how 2 Kings 17 impacted me when I discovered I'd been trying to live for both God and my cherished false gods at the same time. This was as successful as dieting on Sour Patch Kids®, by the way. The Israelites' exile into Assyrian captivity was especially tragic because God had delivered them from the bondage of Egypt earlier in their history. He'd set them free so they could worship and serve Him, not for them to return to captivity. But isn't this what we're so prone to do?

REFRESH YOUR MEMORY FROM YESTERDAY BY READING 2 KINGS 17:7 AND FILLING IN THE BLANK.

"This disaster happened because the people of Israel sinned against the Lord *their God who had brought them out of the land of Egypt from the _____ of Pharaoh king of Egypt and because they worshiped other gods."*

I've felt under the power (hand) of many things in my life. It's been as simple as not being able to pass up another cookie—or seven—after dinner or as consuming as jealousy. Long before the exile we read about yesterday in 2 Kings, the Israelites were under the controlling force of oppressive Pharaohs. In our particular culture, we might find ourselves ruled by alcohol,

Netflix® binges, an unhealthy relationship, unforgiveness, materialism, or sexual addiction. As we learned on Day One, we can also be in bondage to something inherently good that has turned harmful by virtue of how much it consumes us.

As we consider the modern-day idols that hold power over us, today we'll read about one of those Pharaohs who oppressed Israel. Prior to his opposition, the Israelites had flourished in Egypt under the favor of Joseph's influence. But when this new Pharaoh came into power, one who didn't know Joseph, he persecuted the Israelites because he was threatened by their growth.

READ EXODUS 1:1-22; 2:23.

Cite the specific ways Pharaoh oppressed the Israelites.

We live in a world where proud and ruthless rulers still oppress the poor and powerless. Every year I visit a country in Eastern Europe where this kind of oppression is a normal way of life for its people. While unjust leaders still oppress people today, many of us in Western society deal more with pharaohs of the heart. While God delivered Israel from under the power of a physical ruler, the truths of this story apply to the modern-day idols that rule us internally. I can relate to the Israelites' story for many reasons but chief among them has been the discovery that only the hand of the Lord was (and is) strong enough to rescue me. This I'm clear on.

PERSONAL REFLECTION: Reflect on what currently holds power over you. Write down who or what is a pharaoh in your life.

Only the hand of the Lord was and is strong enough to rescue me.

Why does this person or thing hold power over you?

READ EXODUS 2:23-25.

What did the Israelites do as a result of their suffering?

PERSONAL REFLECTION: Write about a time when you felt absolutely powerless in a situation and all you could do was cry out to God.

List the four ways God responded to the Israelites' cries for help (vv. 24-25).

God _____ *their groaning;*

God _____ *His covenant;*

God _____ *the Israelites;*

God _____ .

PERSONAL REFLECTION: Which of God's responses to the Israelites in Exodus 2 means the most to you and why?

When the author of Exodus said that God remembered His covenant, he wasn't implying that God had somehow forgotten the terms of it during the past 430 years while the Israelites were in Egypt, but then suddenly realized He needed to be faithful to His word. The term *remember* in the Old Testament is often associated with God acting at a certain time. It has to do with God determining when it's time to move rather than His recollection of something. Because of God's covenant with Abraham, which would continue to be renewed in every generation, God was about to free the Israelites through a man named Moses.

READ ABOUT GOD'S CALL TO MOSES IN EXODUS 3:1-12.

The Israelites couldn't keep up with the abusive workload. Their baby boys had been executed. They'd been stripped of their freedom. They could do nothing but cry out to God in the midst of their despair. While I've never experienced what the Israelites endured as captives in Egypt, I've known utter powerlessness against debilitating fears, terrifying depression, and idols I've put my hope in that left me bitterly disappointed. I've also walked alongside friends and loved ones in unexplainable circumstances beyond their ability to endure, some of those circumstances which can only be described by the word *oppressive*.

Earlier in today's study you named a false god in your life that's currently holding power over you and why. In a moment I'm going to ask you to describe the ways you've allowed the false God to oppress you. Before we get there though, here's a personal example to stimulate your thinking.

After moving to Nashville in my twenties, I was consumed by the success—or lack thereof—of my music career. My happiness rose and fell on how many records I sold and whether or not the record company believed in me. I missed opportunities to relax and enjoy other aspects of life while trying to control my career. The deceiving element was that the more I tried to control

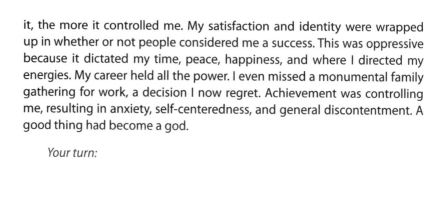

it, the more it controlled me. My satisfaction and identity were wrapped up in whether or not people considered me a success. This was oppressive because it dictated my time, peace, happiness, and where I directed my energies. My career held all the power. I even missed a monumental family gathering for work, a decision I now regret. Achievement was controlling me, resulting in anxiety, self-centeredness, and general discontentment. A good thing had become a god.

Your turn:

The false gods we serve hinder and wound us in many ways, and oftentimes the wounding begins with the power they hold over us—or the power we give them. But we'll get to that later.

Only one Person can do something about the bondage you're in. Only One is able to rescue you. As I write these words I have such hope for you, knowing that the same One who is able to deliver is also the One who hears our cries for help, remembers His everlasting covenant with us, sees our pain, and enters in (Ex. 2:24-25). D. K. Stuart puts it this way, "The exodus did not come about simply because people were in trouble; it was the result of a prayer of lament for rescue to the *only one who could actually do something about it*"[4] (emphasis mine).

PERSONAL REFLECTION: Are you still relying on yourself to conquer what holds power over you? If so, explain.

If you're at the point where you know you're powerless and desire to rely on God, write it in a prayer.

Being free from our idols begins by recognizing our powerlessness against them. Apart from the power of Christ, we're unable to loose ourselves from their hold. Here's the good news: He's eager to set you free.

DAY FOUR
THE IDOLS
WE CREATE

ISAIAH 44:20: Is not this thing in my right hand a lie? (NIV).

The only thing worse than being under the control of something through no fault of my own is being under the control of something I've actually created. It's pain with extra sides of guilt and regret.

Look back at 2 Kings 17:7 and Exodus 1:8-11 from Days Two and Three respectively. In both scenarios the Israelites were in captivity, but only one situation came as a result of their disobedience. Circle the reference that describes that situation.

The Israelites' captivity in Exodus 1 does not appear to be a result of God's punishment, nor is disobedience mentioned. However, the 2 Kings passage paints a different picture. What I'm getting at is that sometimes we find ourselves under the power of something we didn't set out looking for; other times we bring bondage upon ourselves by creating false gods with our own hands. Either way, God desires to set us free.

Today we'll look at a passage in Isaiah that describes a scenario of being under the power of something we've created ourselves. At first glance, this passage may seem absurd to modern readers, but it's more relevant to our day than we may think.

READ ISAIAH 44:6-20.

What types of workers made these idols (vv. 11-13)?

Choose the word that best describes these men:

Tough   Skilled   Smart   Educated

According to verses 9-10, who benefitted from the false gods the workers fashioned?

The workmen who crafted these false gods were skilled professionals who used specific resources to make them, not the least of which was their own strength.

Being talented, skilled, and resourced are blessings we should be intent on cultivating for Christ and His church. The temptation we must resist, however, is using those blessings to create false gods that end up captivating our hearts.

Hold your place in Isaiah 44 and look up 1 Corinthians 10:31. This verse serves as a litmus test for determining how our talents and skills are being used. Regardless of what we do, what should always be our motivation?

PERSONAL RESPONSE: With 1 Corinthians 10:31 in mind, list a few of your skills, talents, resources, or areas of expertise. How can you use these for the glory of God?

SKILLS	HOW THEY GLORIFY GOD

I wonder how our lives would change if we regularly asked ourselves the question, *Am I using my gifts for God's glory or for my own glory, pride, comfort, happiness, or other selfish motive?*

Return to Isaiah 44. Perhaps you had some of the same questions I did: How could anyone think that a god could come from something made with human hands? What power does a lifeless statue of a person set in a temple have? How could the same piece of lumber that's used for firewood also be revered as something that could save? We can clearly see the senseless nature of it all. And yet we'll be surprised over the next few weeks at how often we too look to lifeless things to fulfill us. Before we get there, it's helpful to determine why these skilled workmen—and the worshipers of their idols—had become so deluded.

Am I using my gifts for God's glory or for my own glory, pride, comfort, or happiness?

According to Isaiah 44:18-20, how did the craftsmen arrive at the conclusion that the idols they'd created could save them?

One of the overarching points the Lord is making about a craftsman who thinks he can create a divine being out of earthen material is simply this: It doesn't make any sense! How can the other half of a log you burned in the fire to warm yourself be a savior? How can that same firewood you used to bake bread also be something you worship? The creators of these false gods—and the worshipers of them—had lost their logic and reason.

> They'd arrived at this thinking over time, because their _____ hearts/minds had led them astray (v. 20).

We can all look back at certain times and wonder, *what was I thinking? Where was my common sense? Why couldn't I see the lie in my right hand (Is. 44:20)?* We can almost always point back to being misled by our deceived minds (or deluded hearts).

Deception is often logic based on a faulty premise.

Being deceived is like following an exquisitely crafted compass that has faulty inner workings. We walk in the direction of its misleading arrow, convincing ourselves that our choices are leading us true north. Meanwhile, we're headed deeper and deeper into the woods. We point to our compass— *look, I'm only following the arrow.* But deception is often logic based on a faulty premise.

I'll never be able to read this passage without thinking of a time in my life when I'd allowed myself to be deceived. I'd made a false god out of a person, and I compromised obedience to Jesus for a friendship. I kept trying to mold the truth to fit my desires. In the strangest way, I fully knew my error, but yet had simultaneously convinced myself I was as right as I'd ever been.

PERSONAL REFLECTION: Have you ever been so deceived that you found yourself doing something that made absolutely no sense? If so, briefly describe that situation.

The reason I asked you to recount this time in your life is not to bring you back to a low point—we don't need more lows for lows' sakes. Rather, I hope that by recognizing how you were deceived by a false god, what led up to it, and what made you susceptible to its draw, will better equip you to identify deception in the future.

The worshipers in Isaiah 44 bowed down to their false gods for salvation, help in troubled times, fulfillment, protection from enemies, and provision in lean circumstances. While the objects of their worship were different from the false gods we look to today, the reasons why they worshiped them were in many ways the same.

PERSONAL REFLECTION: Who or what are you putting your hope in to rescue, save, or fulfill you? What are you counting on this object or person to provide?

We know the inside of the compass is broken—however beautiful the outside might be—if its arrow is pointing in a direction different than what is revealed to us in Scripture. We tend to think of deception as something that leads us in the exact opposite direction of God's Word, but oftentimes it's just a few degrees to the left or right. If we let our wayward desires lead, we'll eventually find ourselves miles from where we should be.

PERSONAL RESPONSE: Ask the Lord to show you if you're being deceived, or if there's a lie in your right hand. Confess whatever He reveals to you in the space below.

> I formed you,
> you are my servant;
> Israel, you will never
> be forgotten by me.
> Isaiah 44:21b

Recognizing our false gods will do us little good if we fail to turn from them to the one true God. Finish today's chapter by reading about the God who is above all gods in Isaiah 44:21-23.

PERSONAL RESPONSE: From these verses, what about God's character and deeds mean the most to you and why?

I'm moved by the fact that God "formed" (made) us (v. 21), as opposed to us making Him. The deluded idol-makers worshiped what they'd formed with their own hands, but we worship the One whose hands formed us. Let's acknowledge before our Creator that we are His servants and He is our Redeemer. It's not too late to return to Him (v. 22).

DAY FIVE
FINDING OUR TREASURE

MATTHEW 6:21: For where your treasure is, there your heart will be also.

Let me begin by congratulating you on finishing your first week of homework. I'll admit this study is nothing if not invasive. I can testify that the most difficult seasons of my life were when God came for more of my heart and therefore my false gods. But I wouldn't trade one moment of His loving hand of discipline in my life. The freedom and blessings that resulted have been beyond compare. Hebrews 12:11 reminds us that no discipline is pleasant at the time, but painful. Afterward, however, it yields a harvest of righteousness. I do love a harvest.

READ PROVERBS 4:20-23.

What does verse 23 tell us to do and why?

God gave us these instructions because He created the heart to be the wellspring of life. It's the most central part of our being. It guides, feels, receives, hurts, heals, dreams, connects, loves. So it's not surprising that the most difficult false gods to conquer in our lives are the ones to which we've attached our hearts. The idols that have been the most difficult to root out of my life by far are the ones that have woven themselves into my heart. Jesus spoke about this specifically in the Gospel of Matthew.

READ MATTHEW 6:19-24.

PERSONAL REFLECTION: Why are our hearts and treasure so intimately connected? Take some time to think this through, and write about it in the space provided.

Jesus commanded us to store our treasure in heaven rather than on earth. All our earthly possessions are in a state of breaking down. They're temporal, not even safe from things like moths and rust. Whereas anything we do for Christ will last for eternity and is being stored for us in heaven where no one and nothing can get to it.

I remember visiting dear friends of my parents who are missionaries in Milan, Italy. Joan and her husband Sam left a successful gold business he'd started in the States for the opportunity to plant a church in Milan. I was sitting in their living room, no doubt with an espresso in hand, when Joan mentioned that they'd been robbed twenty-six times over the forty years of serving there. "I don't have one valuable piece of jewelry left," she said with the most gracious laugh. "There's really nothing left to take!"

Joan never denied the pain of losing such meaningful possessions, nor did she offer spiritual platitudes. The plain reality is that the treasures she has stored in heaven include the hundreds, maybe thousands, of Italians who have come to know Jesus Christ as their Lord and Savior because of her witness. These Italians are some of her dearest friends. No thief can snatch those treasures from her the way her earthly ones were stolen.

Neither money nor possessions have moral value in and of themselves. They're neither holy nor evil. The issue is where our hearts are in relationship to them. If our possessions, houses, clothes, cars, and money are our most valuable treasures then they also have our heart's devotion. And if our hearts are devoted to what we have and own, then our treasures become our gods. As Jesus explained, you can't serve both God and your stuff.

What we treasure apart from God is where we'll find our idols.

PERSONAL REFLECTION: According to verse 24, what's wrong with straddling the fence trying to serve both God and our money? Why is this impossible?

Revisit Ken Sande's definition of an idol from Day One of this week. I think we can sum up his definition by saying that what we treasure apart from God is where we'll find our idols.

Fill in the blank from Matthew 6:21. For where your _____ is, there your _____ will be also.

Turn back to Isaiah 44:9. Describe the value of these treasured idols.

READ 2 KINGS 17:15.

Circle the answer that best completes the following sentence. We become like what we:

Follow   Reject   Wish for

As we build on some key verses from this week we come to the following revelations:

- **MATTHEW 6:21:** What we treasure is where our heart is.

- **ISAIAH 44:9:** If we treasure idols, we treasure what is worthless (benefits no one).

- **2 KINGS 17:15:** We become like what we follow.

PERSONAL REFLECTION: When you consider your life, which of the phrases above best relates to the current state of your heart and why?

The bright side of evaluating the treasures of our hearts is that it's the first step in rooting out what's worthless to make room for the One who surpasses our deepest longings and desires.

If God is our treasure, our hearts will be devoted to Him.

If God is our treasure, our hearts will be devoted to Him. If we treasure Him, we're treasuring what is of infinite value. If we follow Him, we will become like Him.

READ 2 CORINTHIANS 3:18.

As I think of being transformed into His likeness, I'm reminded of the positive meaning of becoming like what we worship.

PERSONAL REFLECTION: Ponder the ways you practically follow, and therefore worship, the Lord and how these ways have molded you into His image.

Obedience to the Word
Serve @ church
personal Bible time
worship

You've done a lot of heart work this week. You've studied what false gods look like in our modern culture, realizing you may deal with more idolatry than you initially thought. You dug into 2 Kings 17 and were made aware of how easy it is to say you love God while living for lots of other things. You spent some time with the Israelites in the Book of Exodus, remembering the bondage they endured under the reign of Pharaoh and how the one true God set them free. You then turned to Isaiah 44 and discovered that some of the worst gods we find ourselves in bondage to are often the ones we've created ourselves. In other words, you've had a light-hearted skip through the Old Testament confronting your modern-day idolatry, in case you were wondering how to categorize your experience.

In all seriousness, this is where freedom begins. As you root out the idols of your heart you'll be making room for God to dwell. For the sake of emphasis, write the words *make room* in the margin. This phrase will serve as our two-word reminder of what we hope to accomplish over these eight weeks together. Nothing, and I do mean nothing, will rival who God will be to you and what He will do for you when you make Him the treasure of your heart.

SESSION TWO VIEWER GUIDE

FREE TO WORSHIP

GROUP DISCUSSION

What one thing from this video teaching really resonated with you? Why?

How does the phrase *functional god* help you think differently about the prevalence of false gods in your life? How are functional gods affecting you?

According to Kelly's teaching from Exodus, why does God long for us to be free from our false gods?

Kelly said, "We can only worship God to the degree that we are free." What did she mean?

Are you living your life unencumbered for God and His purposes? If so, how? If not, why not?

Have you ever tried to bring your worship into Egypt or Egypt into your worship? Explain.

Video sessions available for purchase or rent at **LIFEWAY.COM/NOOTHERGODS**

Cilantro Black Beans and Rice (serves 6-8)

INGREDIENTS:

4 (15-ounce) cans of black beans

2 cups whole grain brown rice

½ yellow onion

1 bunch fresh cilantro

6 garlic cloves

1 tablespoon olive oil

12 ounces shredded Monterey Jack cheese, divided

2 avocados, sliced

1 jar salsa

1 cup sour cream

1 bag tortilla chips

I don't know what it is about this recipe that gives you all the joy of comfort food while still being mostly healthy. And if you want to go from mostly healthy to totally healthy, you can hold the cheese, sour cream, and chips. But then you lose the fun! I say go comfort food and mostly healthy, and then feel really good about the whole meal. You will love this dish and come back to it again and again.

DIRECTIONS

Preheat your oven to 325 degrees.

Heat black beans in a saucepan over medium-high heat, keeping most of the juice from the cans. In a separate pot, prepare rice according to package instructions, and set aside. Chop onion and cilantro. Mince garlic. Warm olive oil in a sauté pan over medium heat, approximately 1 minute. Sauté onion, cilantro, and garlic in oil. Allow beans to warm for 20 minutes, then stir the onion mixture into the black beans.

Pour black bean concoction into a 13x9-inch pan, and top with 8 ounces of shredded cheese, covering extensively. Cover with aluminum foil, and bake for 30 minutes.

Serve black bean entrée over rice alongside a nice spread of avocado slices, salsa, sour cream, tortilla chips, and the remaining shredded cheese for a beautiful presentation.

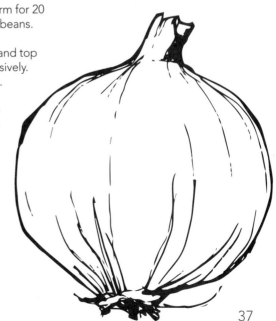

THE WHY BEHIND OUR IDOLS

One of the greatest surprises I've had since first writing *No Other Gods* came when my brother David called to tell me he had a job interview in Nashville. At the time, he and his family were living in Northern Virginia where we grew up. Prior to this conversation, David and I would talk on the phone approximately twice every seven years. I chalk this up to him not being a big phone talker, and possibly to the fact that during our childhood I tortured him ever so slightly. So when he called to tell me about his job interview, it went like this:

"Hey Kel, how's it going?"

"Hey David, I'm good. Great to hear from you! How are you?"

"Oh, you know, doing pretty well. What's going on with you?"

"Why are you calling me?"

A few weeks later, David was offered the job. He and his wife, Megen, and their two small children, Will and Harper, moved exactly 2.8 miles down the road from me. (Aunts keep track of these metrics.) Having them close by has been one of the most fantastic blessings of my adult life. Plus, they recently added another girl to their adorable brood, meaning I now have a Nashville niece from scratch. I've got car seats in my SUV and juice boxes in the fridge—I'm owning aunthood.

One of the little-known qualifications for being an aunt of young children is that you're expected to know the answer to every conceivable question: Why does God give us dreams at night? Why can't my room be full of pickles so I'll never be hungry? Why is mommy's tummy so huge when babies are so small? Kids ask questions (sometimes offensive ones) at an abnormally swift rate. It's as if they're trying to meet a secret quota we adults know nothing about. They intuitively understand that on the other side of the question "why?" could be an answer that opens up their world.

Sometimes I wish I were this curious, this relentlessly inquisitive about the things that perplex me and sometimes keep me stuck. While we as adults can overdo it on the question of why—dwelling on our pasts to the detriment of the gifts in front of us—we do well to consider why we're drawn to our personal false gods and what's at the root of our idolatry. Once we know the why behind our idols we can take our hatchets to those roots, striking them where it counts.

When I first moved to Nashville as a singer/songwriter, I had my heart set on fame and success. In some areas of my life, my glory was more important to me than the Lord's, making my desire for success an idol. It wasn't until I considered why a thriving career in music had become all-consuming to me that I realized what my heart was really after: securing friends who I thought would make me happy. That was my true longing, far more than having fame for fame's sake.

Once I understood that what I really wanted were friends—but wrongly thought they would only want me if I were successful—I realized I'd set an inordinate amount of pressure on certain people to meet my needs and fulfill my desires. I saw a successful music career as the way to keep those relationships serviced and working for me. Even though this thinking was flawed, at least I was gaining clarity on what my idols truly were. It was then that God began to mend my places of shame and insecurity, establish my worth in Him, and teach me how to cultivate healthy friendships that were true and lasting, not based on the fleeting nature of celebrity and fortune.

I could give you several more examples of false gods that gripped me for reasons I didn't understand at first. Asking the Lord for wisdom to reveal why I'm drawn to certain false gods has illumined my path to true healing over and over again. As you prepare for this week's study, I encourage you to ask the Lord questions with the expectation of a child. Ask the Holy Spirit to show you the lies you believe about your false gods, the reasons you're drawn to those gods, and the broken and empty places in your life that make you especially vulnerable to them. You may be surprised by what's at the root of your idolatry and why you've given your idols such power over you. Far better still, the One who knows the why knows the way to freedom. He came to show you that way.

DAY ONE

FINDING
OUR IDENTITY

DEUTERONOMY 7:6b: The LORD your God has chosen
you out of all the peoples on the face of the earth
to be his people, his treasured possession (NIV).

When I first wrote this study more than a decade ago, the girls
and I nicknamed ourselves the NOGS for *No Other Gods*.
Because we were clever like that. I made the mistake of sharing
this tidbit in the original study, and it caught on like Bible
study wildfire. I've met fellow NOGS from all over the country,
including a group I hugged at a Southern California church
where I recently spoke. They said they were the SoCal NOGS
and their husbands were the HOGS. I'm not sure what to do
about this. However, if I had it to do all over again I might not
have started all this nogsense. Keeping it real, folks.

Last week we identified what idols are, both broadly and personally. This
week we'll look at the why behind them. We'll consider questions such as,
*why do we choose idols? Why are they appealing to us? Why are they so hard to
resist or give up?* This is one of my favorite parts of our study because we get
to uncloak the mystery of our idols' allure. We get to unveil what our hearts
are truly after. This is all important because if we can get to the why of idols,
we can get to the root of them. Which is important so we can …

> *List the two words you wrote in the margin at the end of Day Five last
> week (p. 35).*

The first two times the original NOGS met, we gathered for less of a study
and more of a focus group. I wanted to know what was propelling us toward
the many functional gods we had in our lives. The collective answer I heard
in the living room of my old condo is the same one I've been getting over
the past ten years: We often look to things or people to find our identities.
I was surprised our original Nashville group gave this as an answer, given
that Alli, Lauri, Carrie, and Anadara were all married at the time (and still
are). For some reason I thought that trying to find one's identity was more
of a single-person thing—not so much an anyone thing.

*We often look to things
or people to find our
identities.*

I've since realized that regardless of one's marital status we're all caught in a pursuit to discover our identities. And it's not just people in their twenties and thirties. According to many of my older friends, finding identity can be a lifelong struggle, one that changes at different points in a person's life. Husbands don't seem to solve it. Kids apparently don't satisfy it. Careers fall short—I can speak directly to this one. Even our ministries can't give us the identities we're looking for. Come to think of it, I can speak to this one as well.

and how we are trained / taught to think they will :(

One of the familiar Christian clichés of our day is that we should find our identities in Christ. However, I'm not sure we always know what that phrase means. My hope is that today's passage will help us better understand what the statement means by seeing what it doesn't mean. We're going to revisit the Israelites during a time of identity crisis, helping us better understand why we often look to false gods to find our identities.

READ 1 SAMUEL 8:1-22.

According to verses 7-8, what were the people guilty of?

forsook God   rejected God
serving other gods

List everything that motivated the Israelites to ask for a king (vv. 5,20).

wanted to be like the other nations; wanted someone to fight for them

What did Samuel warn would happen if their request was granted (vv. 10-18)?

God would not answer them.

Then we will be like all the other nations, with a king to lead us and to go out before us and fight our battles.
1 Samuel 8:20

Nothing good can come from this list. Everyone is in big trouble if this list materializes. Yet the Israelites wouldn't listen; their minds were made up. They wanted a king for the most insignificant reason—so they could be like everyone else. Sounds familiar.

PERSONAL REFLECTION: What do you currently have your heart set on because it's something "everyone else" has? (This can be a thing, person, status, and so forth.) How do you think it will improve your identity?

Husband
Secure job / $ stability   >   loved
                                  happy
                                  comfortable

NOW READ DEUTERONOMY 7:6-8.

What was Israel's identity before they went looking for a king?

God

The Israelites already had an astounding identity. They were the chosen people of God. But when they forsook God for the prominent idols of their day, they lost sight of what they had and most importantly, who they were.

When I was first writing this study my friend Lauri sent me an email about an '80s rerun she was watching that tied into today's passage. (Because, you know, Deuteronomy and '80s reruns so clearly go together.) In light of our study on identity, she recapped the scene of a father meeting his daughter's boyfriend for the first time.

The father asked the boyfriend what his plans were. The boyfriend replied, "Well, I thought I'd spend some time just trying to find myself." The father asked, "How much time do you think it will take?" The boyfriend answered, "About five or ten years." To which the father replied, "Well, you'll be able to find yourself plus a couple more people, won't you?"

Later, when his daughter asked him, "So? How do you like him?," the father said, "I don't know if that's him or not. He hadn't found himself."[1]

As a child I didn't understand this exchange. But as an adult, I get the humor precisely because I sometimes struggle with who I am and where I fit, even though I think I should know myself pretty well by now. In the same way, the Israelites would only find themselves by realizing that God had already found them. They already had an identity as God's chosen people.

READ 1 PETER 2:9-12, KEEPING 1 SAMUEL 8 IN MIND.

How does this passage describing New Testament believers in Jesus compare to what we just read about the Israelites?

Which words does Peter use to describe the friends he's writing to in verse 11?

BELOVED! Sojourners/exiles

PERSONAL REFLECTION: In what ways are you living as though this world is your permanent residence, finding your identity in what it has to offer?

By focusing on the success I can get in this world & having enough money for the next 60-80 yrs. Worrying about opinion of others.

Strangers, aliens, peculiar people—growing up in a Christian home, none of these words sounded exciting to me. I didn't always like being the weird kid because I wasn't allowed to watch a certain movie or because I went to youth group on Wednesday nights, or because my dad was a pastor. Words like *peculiar* and *alien* weren't what I was shooting for in the senior superlatives. But as an adult these concepts have shifted for me. I'm more convinced than ever before that the things the world finds its identity in—wealth, fame, romance, position, fashion, pleasure, fitness, power—are fleeting and unsatisfying identity markers. These things can't define me, nor can they give me a fulfilling and lasting idea of my worth.

Peter's descriptions on the other hand are valuable markers of who we are in Christ:

❏ *A chosen race (generation)*

im not a mistake. Im not overlooked.

❏ *A royal priesthood*

❏ *A holy nation* despite my beh/thoughts, God still sees me as HOLY.

❏ *A people for His possession*

God cares and pursues me more than any man will ever.

❏ *Called out of darkness and into His light*

my deliverer & rescuer. nothing can separate me.

❏ *God's people*

❏ *Having received mercy*

Next to each description, briefly write how each one affects your identity. For instance, knowing that I'm part of God's royal priesthood gives me confidence as I minister to people individually and within the context of the church. Knowing that I've received mercy keeps me humble and grateful for what the Lord has done in my life.

In verse 12, Peter qualifies his statement about us being peculiar strangers. We'll be strange and alien-like because our good works for Jesus will stand out as so breathtakingly good and different and selfless that those around us can't help but praise God. The extreme goodness of our lives is the peculiar part, setting us apart in distinctive ways.

What does Peter say will obscure this goodness (v. 11)?

passions of the FLESH.

Fulfilling our sinful desires will snuff out the bright flame of this burning goodness. By indulging our sinful desires we actually become the reverse of peculiar and strange—we become normal. If you're seeking true individualism and distinctiveness, chasing your lusts will only make you like everyone else, with little of your Christlike identity showing. The Lord wants you to stand out, not for the sake of your own individualism, but for the beauty of His glory. Who Jesus has called you to be is the most exciting and liberating identity you can have.

Who Jesus has called you to be is the most exciting and liberating identity you can have.

Today, we examined the futility of trying to find our identities in a king (or anything else), while discovering the fulfillment of knowing our identities in Christ. For Israel, Saul (their first king) was not a good god, <u>nor was having a king the answer to their identity crisis.</u> In contrast, for you as a believer in Jesus, how wonderful if it were said of you: *The goodness of Jesus Christ burns so brightly in her that she almost seems from another world. People can't help but turn their attention to God after being around her.* This is the kind of stranger I want to be and the kind Peter was referring to.

PERSONAL RESPONSE: What's currently obscuring your identity in Christ? Take some time to journal about this. After naming those things, write how dealing with those sins will expose your God-given goodness and give you a better sense of your true identity in Him.

> Wanting to belong, yet my experiences affirm that its difficult.
> pride — bc of my lack of cnxn to people wanting to overcompensate & be "better"

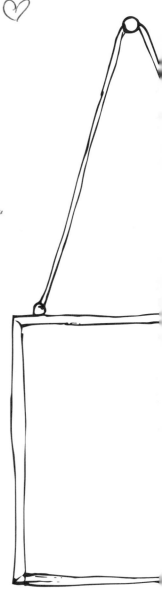

Through Christ, you are part of His chosen people. You're part of the royalty of God, holy in His sight. You belong to Him forever and ever. You've received mercy, you live in His light, and you have what you need to minister to others. This is your identity.

MEETING A NEED

GENESIS 16:11b: The LORD has heard your cry of affliction.

Need. Many of us run to idols because we're convinced they'll meet our needs. We have an interesting narrative to read today so we'll get right to it—the story of Sarah (a.k.a. Sarai) and Hagar.

READ GENESIS 16:1-15.

Note the indications of gnawing needs you detect in the characters.

When I read Scripture my heart is often most penetrated by small phrases, which is why I encourage a slow reading of a text. A pair of words slowly pondered can be more meaningful than a quick read of an entire book.

According to verse 2, what did Sarah perceive as a need?

need to have children

Sarah and Hagar lived in an era that prized the family. For a woman of that time, bearing children was viewed as essential to her worth and legacy. If you weren't married or couldn't have children, your value in society suffered a near deathblow.

What was Sarah's remedy to her problem?

give her servant to her husband & have a son. Child.

Finish verse 2: "Since the LORD has prevented me from bearing children, go to my slave; perhaps through her I can ___obtain children by her___*."*

The phrase you just wrote down was a life changer for me. Even after I'd read that passage countless times, I had never considered Hagar an idol of Sarah's. Not until I read the simple phrase, "Perhaps through her I can build a family." (Some of your translations will say "obtain children.") In those days it might as well have read, "Perhaps through her I can build a *life*."

Think about the irony of this situation: Sarah, a woman who'd been chosen by the God of Israel was looking to an Egyptian slave girl to give her life meaning. She was depending on the lowest of the low, as far as the social standing of that time was concerned. Then the very person she thought could meet her need would be the one she'd end up hating. This is often the case for us—think of any kind of addiction.

Sarah's dependence on Hagar leads me to ask the obvious question: Other than God, through what or _whom_ are you trying to build a life? I've intentionally asked this question a few times in different ways throughout our study. It can take a while for our eyes to be opened to our false gods, so coming at it from different angles is helpful. If you feel you have a new answer based on today's reading, answer the Personal Reflection below.

PERSONAL REFLECTION: Other than God, through whom or what are you trying to build a life?

a husband — "then my life can truly begin"

LET'S GO BACK IN TIME AND READ ABOUT A PROMISE GOD GAVE ABRAHAM (A.K.A. ABRAM) AND HIS FAMILY. READ GENESIS 15:1-6.

PERSONAL TAKE: Based on God's promise to Abraham and his family, why do you think Sarah tried to fulfill this promise on her own? Why did she feel the need to help God out?

her TIMING didn't match Gods. She doubted God's miracles could happen in her old age.

PERSONAL REFLECTION: Describe a time you were convinced you had to fix something on your own because God wasn't moving fast enough for you or in the way you hoped He would.

Getting into grad school   _Marriage, Having kids_
Getting a good paying Job.

We think that when we manipulate and control our situations by relying on false gods, we're the only ones affected. But look at the damage done in Genesis 16 because Sarah determined to meet her need her way.

Who was negatively affected by Sarah's decision and how?

Hagar, Ishmael, Abram
↳ felt hated, isolated   _↳ had child who would not truly be his heir_

NOW READ GENESIS 21:1-6.

We saw what happened when Sarah tried to build a family her own way through Hagar. Sarah wasn't the only one who suffered. But in Genesis 21 we see that God had a plan from the beginning for how this story would unfold. His plan would happen with or without Hagar, with or without Ishmael, with or without Sarah's manipulation, and with or without Abraham's passivity. But how much more peaceful and blessed the situation would have been if

Sarah had trusted in and waited on the Lord to fulfill His promise instead of manipulating the circumstances.

When God doesn't meet the very real needs we're living with on our timetable and terms, we tend to complicate the process. We often abandon trust in the one true God and turn to the foreign slave girl. Granted, things looked bleak for Sarah: She'd genuinely suffered through barrenness, was helpless to give her husband what they both desired in a family, and was unable to carry on her legacy, all while bearing the shame of not having what everyone else had. But God had a miraculous plan for her despite the circumstances. Sarah had genuine need. But at the point of our need is always the point where our faith is tested. If we can do it ourselves it doesn't require God.

Certainly Sarah had waited a long time for a "life." But God fully intended to give that to her. Not through Hagar. Not through Abraham. Not through her scheming. But through Himself. We of course know He fulfilled this promise in Isaac. This truth encourages me to wait for God and keep my anxious hands off the process. That doesn't mean I sit around; there's plenty to do. It just means I don't try to force the outcome.

PERSONAL REFLECTION: In what situation are you trying to meet a need through a false god? Are you looking to this functional god because you don't believe God can ultimately meet your need? Explain.

PERSONAL RESPONSE: How does Sarah's story encourage you to wait for God's perfect timing in meeting your needs? What steps can you take to turn from the "slave girls"* of idolatry to the one true God?

Be reminded through these examples
Pray

*(The slave girl "Hagar" was deeply valued by God. We see His love for her in sending His angel to meet her in her most hopeless hour. Still, the principle remains that Sarah was looking to the lesser of this world to remedy her problem instead of to her God.)

DAY THREE
NUMBING OUR PAIN

1 SAMUEL 1:27b: The LORD has granted me
what I asked of him (NIV).

Sitting at a restaurant across from a friend who works with troubled adolescents, I asked her why she thought the kids she counseled looked to the false gods of sex, alcohol, drugs, and other addictions. She simply said, "to take away their pain."

This week we've looked at our propensity to run to idols because we're seeking an identity in them and because we hope they'll meet our needs. Today we'll look at the reason my friend gave me—we want our false gods to take away our pain. But in today's text, instead of finding someone who sought an idol in her suffering, we'll look at someone whose pain drove her to God. Who couldn't use a success story?

Name something in your life that you'd like to change but are unable to change left only to your own devices.

physical health issues / body
singleness

READ 1 SAMUEL 1:1-18, AND LOOK FOR ALL THE INFERENCES OF PAIN IN HANNAH'S LIFE.

Hannah's obvious and foremost source of pain was her barrenness. But I think some lesser-discussed pains are important to note.

Hannah's husband, Elkanah, had another wife named Peninnah (translation: things are off to a rocky start). How did Peninnah treat Hannah?

provoked her
irritated her

How long did this persist (v. 7)?

every year – all the time

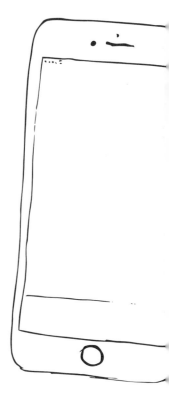

What state did Eli the priest think Hannah was in when he saw her praying in the Lord's house?

drunk

Hannah's pain continued to mount through chapter 1. She was sharing her husband. She couldn't bear children. Her husband's other wife provoked her and had the one thing she wanted—children. The priest accused her of being drunk in the house of the Lord. Yet I see another problem in Hannah's life, one much bigger than any of the others.

Who had closed Hannah's womb (vv. 5-6)?

GOD.

In a sense, God was Hannah's biggest problem. It wasn't infertility, Peninnah, Elkanah, or Eli. I've found this revelation to be both troubling and full of comfort. Troubling because God is credited with closing Hannah's womb, which is difficult to reconcile from our vantage point. Comforting because we see that even our suffering is guided by and covered in God's loving hands.

Even our suffering is guided by and covered in God's loving hands.

PERSONAL TAKE: This is a hard question. Why do you think God purposely allows and/or brings pain into our lives?

To show us who is truly in control, test our faith

Look back at verses 15-16. How did Hannah deal with her pain and the unanswerable questions of her barrenness?

praying

Hannah's predicament of barrenness—and at the hand of God—appears a prime opportunity for her to run to an idol for relief. But let's keep going.

READ 1 SAMUEL 1:19-27.

Did Hannah find relief in her soul before or after she became pregnant (v. 18)? Why is this significant?

Before

I want to finish today's study by having you meditate on Hannah's prayer.

SLOWLY READ 1 SAMUEL 2:1-11.

PERSONAL TAKE: Which of these eleven verses means the most to you right now and why?

V.8 raises up the poor — lifts the needy — to make them sit with princes and inherit seat of honor.

I never felt like I belonged, but this reminds me that God sees me and knows my heart & will bring me up w/ Him

How many times is Samuel's name mentioned in the prayer? (Circle the correct answer.)

4   2   (0)   7

Hannah was so taken with the Lord that Samuel isn't even mentioned in her prayer. I'm always so moved by this. Her deepest desire in having a son was overshadowed by God and His power and goodness. God as the blesser, is always greater than the blessing.

God as the blesser is always greater than the blessing.

PERSONAL REFLECTION: How was Hannah's life enriched by the pain she suffered?

Is there a time of personal pain or suffering in your past that you look back on now with joy and/or peace? Explain.

College – deep loneliness/depression – but a place where I met God, heard from God, felt on a journey that despite being w/o friends, God was all I needed. So grateful.

You may be in a place of deep pain, grief, and loneliness. You may be wondering if God has forgotten you or grappling with why He's allowed or caused the hardship you're walking through. Hannah dealt with all of these questions. Yet instead of turning to the false gods of her day, she continued to go to the house of the Lord. She poured out her pain to the Lord, and she feasted in His house. In this week's video teaching session I'll share more in detail about Hannah's life. You won't want to miss the encouragement from her story.

TURN TO PHILIPPIANS 4:19.

What will God supply (or meet) according to the riches of Christ Jesus?

→ EVERY need of mine. Amen! ←

Life can be hard and complicated. Sometimes God meets our needs differently than we think He will or should. We may ache for a certain outcome while God is providing for us in ways we can't always see or understand. So when I don't know how to pray about my own needs or the needs of others, I pray Philippians 4:19. I claim its promise. For if you could pile together the world's beauty, treasures, and wealth, God's riches in Christ Jesus would make them look like an ant hill.

Thank you Lord!

PERSONAL RESPONSE: One of my favorite descriptions of Hannah is that she poured out her heart to the Lord (1 Sam. 1:15). In light of Philippians 4:19, spend some time pouring your heart out to the Lord about whatever need or unresolved questions you have. Feel free to journal your prayer and other significant thoughts.

DAY FOUR
WHEN GOD
IS SILENT

EXODUS 24:3b: Everything the LORD has said we will do (NIV).

Identity. Need. Pain. These are just a few of the catalysts behind our search for false gods. But what about something more vague? What about God's silence? Often when the Lord is quiet or not acting on our behalf in the way we thought or hoped He would, we decide we're on our own. We justify a functional god here, an idol there, because after all, where is God? At least the false god we're looking to in place of Him is present with us.

Today we'll revisit the Israelites since their journey—mistakes and successes—is an example for us.

After God delivered the Israelites from their bondage in Egypt, He called Moses to meet with Him on Mount Sinai to give Moses the Ten Commandments.

READ EXODUS 24:12-18.

What did Moses tell the elders to do while he was gone?
(Mark the correct answer.)
❏ *Prepare an altar for the Lord*
❏ *Make alternate plans in case he didn't come back*
☑ *Wait for him*
❏ *Make a golden calf*

How long was Moses up on the mountain (v. 18)?

40 days; 40 nights

READ EXODUS 32:1.

Why did the people seek new gods to go before them?

Because Moses had not yet returned to them.

Moses was a mediator between Israel and God. Moses spoke directly with the Lord and then passed on His messages to the people. If Moses was out of pocket, it was almost as if God had disappeared as well. Though I don't believe God ever truly removes His presence from us (Ps. 139:7-10), we see places in Scripture where God was silent, or darkness obscured His presence for different purposes. Sometimes His felt absence was sin related, and other times it appears to be used as a test or growth period for His children.

Take for example Exodus 33:3 when God threatened not to go with the Israelites because they were stiff-necked. In a much different situation found in Job 23:8, a righteous man named Job lamented that no matter where he went he couldn't find God.

Sometimes we sense God more palpably in our lives than at others times. When His presence feels more distant, if not completely gone, we must resist the temptation to substitute the tangible things that we can touch and feel for the God we temporarily can't sense.

READ EXODUS 32:2-5.

What did the Israelites do to remedy their situation?
(Mark the correct answer.)
❏ *Waited for Moses*
❏ *Fasted for Moses to return*
❏ *Asked Aaron to take Moses' place*
☑ *Asked Aaron to make them gods*

Where did Aaron get the gold to make the calf?
from the people

Clearly the people didn't do what Moses had instructed the elders to do, which was wait for him to return. Instead, they got antsy and asked Aaron to make them new gods. He agreed, casting a golden calf from their gold earrings.

I know what you're thinking. How could the Israelites do this? Moses, sent by God and with the power of God, had delivered them from the captivity of the Egyptians. They'd seen Moses work a host of miracles such as turning water into blood. They watched him raise his staff and the sea split in two. They walked across on dry ground and then watched while the waters closed up on the Egyptians behind them. But all that was a little while ago, and they hadn't seen Moses for a few weeks. So they started wondering, *maybe Aaron could come up with a new god for us.*

It's easy to look at the Israelites and wonder how in the world they got there so fast. But when was the last time the Lord did something in your life, something you knew was from Him, and within days, weeks, or months you faced a new situation wondering where He was? You found yourself quickly looking to someone or something other than the Lord Almighty to step in and help you.

PERSONAL REFLECTION: Think back to a time when the Lord clearly intervened in your life. What did He reveal about His character then that you've stopped trusting Him for now?

TURN TO EXODUS 3:21-22 AND 12:35-36.

From where did the Israelites get their gold earrings for the golden calf?

neighbors and women living w/ them.

Who made the Egyptians favorably disposed to give the Israelites that gold? *God gave them favor, they trusted them*

Let this penetrate your heart: The Israelites turned God's gifts into gods. The thought of the Israelites taking the very gold that God had given them as a blessing and using that gold to create objects of worship is particularly grievous. How easy it is for us to take the good gifts of people and possessions that God has generously given us, and then turn them into the most sacred affections of our hearts.

PERSONAL RESPONSE: What gifts of God have you turned into something you live for, depend on, or can't live without?

God gave the Israelites gold as earrings and they turned that same gold into a calf. The gold was the same, but its function dramatically changed. This reminds me of the definition of a false god we looked at last week that described how even some of the good things in our lives can become detrimental when they take the place of God.

As you move into a closing prayer, consider this A. W. Tozer quote from the *The Pursuit of God:* "Sin has introduced complications and has made those very gifts of God a potential source of ruin to the soul."[2]

We can only deal with the false gods that take up space in our lives by allowing God to treat our hearts.

You've probably noticed that I often end our lessons with a prayer or a personal reflection. This is because we can only deal with the false gods that take up space in our lives by allowing God to treat our hearts.

PERSONAL RESPONSE: Spend time in prayer confessing the gifts you've turned into false gods. Ask God to show you how to put them in their proper places. Then thank Him for those gifts He's given you.

DAY FIVE
THE GUARD
OF FEAR

JOSHUA 1:9b: Do not be afraid or discouraged, for the LORD
your God is with you wherever you go.

I've been pondering something this week concerning today's
study: *Is fear itself an idol or is it the tie that attaches us to our
idols?* Initially I thought of fear as a false god because of its
power to rule us, drive our decisions, and dictate our actions.
Fear motivates, therefore it must be an idol. Or so I thought.

As I continued pondering, I realized that fear isn't something we want in
our lives; no one likes to be afraid. It's unlike the gods of materialism, sex,
power, and money, which bring us pleasure for a season. We don't seek
after fear. On the contrary, we drown our fears with the likes of alcohol
and entertainment. We avoid our fears through escape and denial. We're
afraid of being afraid. So perhaps fear isn't a primary god but the guard that
stands outside the castle where the primary god lives. In other words, fear
protects our idols.

I've always been afraid of being abandoned. I'm not totally sure what this
springs from, but I started fighting the fear of being left alone as a three
year old, the day my mom dropped me off at preschool. I was petrified.
Not to mention that learning was low on my priority list at that point.
I carried this fear of being left alone into my adulthood. If I'm not diligently
guarding against it, I can allow others to control me because I'm afraid
that if I don't meet their needs or please them they'll leave me, and I'll
ultimately be alone.

In this situation, my true idol is basing my security on people. The fear of
not having this security is not the idol but what attaches me to my idol.
I contend that if we separate our fear from our idols, we can expose what is
actually ruling us. We will clearly see that fear is the agent hired by our idols ✳
to keep us attached. Here's my condensed version: Fear itself is not the god;
the object of our fear is the god.

✳ *Fear itself is not the
god; the object of our
fear is the god.*

How does fear play into one of your main functional gods?

It causes me to run towards my false idol even
more ($)

Are you afraid to leave this idol behind? If so, what are you afraid will happen and why?

I won't have control.

Do not be startled or afraid. Have I not told you and declared it long ago? You are my witnesses! Is there any God but me? There is no other Rock; I do not know any.
Isaiah 44:8

Fear is the single most debilitating and paralyzing emotion I've experienced, and it's one of the most effective weapons the enemy uses against us. It's kept me from doing right things I wanted to do and propelled me to do wrong things I didn't want to do. All because I was afraid of a certain outcome. But as my trust in the Lord has grown deeper my fears have grown dimmer. The more I get to know Christ's character, meditate on the promises of His Word, and walk through challenges where He's proven faithful, the less I'm afraid. One of my closest friends said to me a few years ago, "You really don't deal with fear much do you?" I looked at her like, *This is no time for sarcasm.* But I realized she wasn't kidding. She'd seen God do a true work in my heart over the years, to the point where she'd forgotten fear was once a debilitating foe.

Scripture is especially effective in combatting our fears, not because it dismisses the things we fear, but because it reveals who God is in the midst of those fears. The Lord knows better than anyone that His creation is prone to being afraid. He's intimately acquainted with our frailty. He's aware of what causes our blood to run cold. He knows that panic and anxiety can be our baseline over trust and peace. Perhaps this is why the most often repeated command in both the Old and New Testaments is "do not fear."

I've provided several Scripture references that deal with an assortment of fears. I deliberately kept this day short so you'll have plenty of time to spend in God's Word. I can attest that nothing will calm your fears or reorient your thoughts regarding your fears like the holy Scriptures.

Slowly read the verses on the next page and describe the antidotes given for fear in each situation. Commit to going through all of these in one sitting. As you read the passages, circle the references that are especially meaningful to you. (Note that each verse sits within a larger context that gives a fuller meaning to that particular verse. As you have time over the next few weeks, I encourage you to do a deeper study around the verses that meant the most to you.)

SCRIPTURE	ANTIDOTE
JOSHUA 1:9	no need to fear - God is w/ us. so be strong/ courageous.
PSALM 56:3-4	we can trust God.
✗ PSALM 91:1-5	God protects us all around. Fortress. Refuge - Covering
PSALM 112:6-8	Bad news can't scare us be God keeps us planted firm.
PROVERBS 3:25-26	God is our confidence despite terror / wickedness
ISAIAH 8:11-13	don't fear what anyone else fears. Lord should be your only fear.
ISAIAH 44:8	God is w/us. Our rock. No need to fear.
ISAIAH 51:12-13	comforter. why fear man?
MATTHEW 17:5-8	Jesus is w/ us always - have no fear.
MARK 5:35-36	Believe. No need to fear.
✳ JOHN 6:16-20	Don't be afraid of "rough water"
JOHN 14:25-27	
ACTS 18:9-10	
1 PETER 3:13-15	
1 JOHN 4:18	

PERSONAL REFLECTION: You already circled the references that were most meaningful to you. What fears did they speak to and how can you use these truths to combat those fears?

fear of death.
need sense of safety.

PERSONAL RESPONSE: Speak your fears out loud to the Lord and then read the corresponding Scriptures out loud. Voicing your confessions along with the truth of God's Word is a powerful practice because it allows you to take the fears that have been festering internally and bring them into the light of God's presence and peace.

Today's homework is not meant to totally abolish your fears in one sitting. Sometimes that happens, but being rid of certain fears in your life may be an ongoing work of the Spirit. Hopefully, this study has made you aware of how your fears are entangled with the false gods you're confronting. It's something we'll continue to address.

I'm so thankful you've chosen to do the hard work of facing your fears today. As you continue to face them, the modern-day idols that hold the most power over you will soon lose their grip, and the Lord who tells us "do not fear" will be lifted high and proven trustworthy. I don't want you to miss the abundant life Jesus has called you to because fear is holding you back. Step forward, dear sister. Do not be afraid. For the Lord your God is with you wherever you go.

9-12-19

(ask God!)

HANNAH

Why do we turn to anything else?

→→ am I not doing something or is it not God's timing?

I samuel 1:1-8

Hannah's PAIN →→

1. Crux of her pain: Hannah was childless (Penninah)
2. Pain upon pain - Rival taunted her (Penninah)
3. Place of her pain - on the way to the house of the Lord (v.7)
4. Duration of her pain - year after year (v.8)

"why wont you eat?"

Deut. 12:7, 12

→ Hannah feels excluded, doesn't feel like she belongs...
→ Forsake the presence of the Lord, shut self out.

①. Never stop eating in the house of the Lord, despite your "year to year"

→ Don't stop engaging.

* ②. No single person can fulfill the deepest desires of my ♡.
③. It's only in your "year to year" that God truly becomes the LORD ALMIGHTY!

GROUP DISCUSSION

"remembering" is always followed by God's ACTING.

Hannah 1st person in history to call God "LORD"!
↓
uses it the "Yahweh"

What one thing from this video teaching really resonated with you? Why? ④ Only God can turn yr/after yr PAIN into year after year BLESSING!!

Do you ever "forsake eating at the Lord's table" because you don't feel that you fit or are worthy? Do you disqualify yourself because of heartbreak, grief, or disappointment with God? Explain.

How does Hannah's turning to the LORD Almighty (LORD of Armies) before her pain was resolved encourage you to continue to press into Him in your difficulties?

To what substitute, instead of the Lord, have you run to try and fill the desires of your heart?

Hannah's prayer 2:1-2 is about the BLESSER not the BLESSING!

Discuss a time when you felt "remembered" by God.

Why are we so hesitant to be a person who collapses in the house of the Lord?

When have you had a "year after year" pain become an "each year" blessing? ⑤ Your joy in him with SURPASS the blessing!

Sun-dried Tomato and Feta Pasta (serves 4 generously)

INGREDIENTS:

1 pound (16 ounces) bowtie pasta

1 pound skinless, boneless chicken breasts

2-3 tablespoons olive oil

1 garlic head (about 10 cloves), minced

2 packages sun-dried tomatoes, softened
   according to package instructions and cut
   into strips

½ cup pine nuts

16 ounces feta cheese, crumbled

1 (16-ounce) can pitted black olives, chopped

Salt and black pepper, to taste

We all need a go-to pasta dish we can count on for comfort, ease, and exceptional flavor. You can throw this dish together last minute for your family and friends, or dress it up for a dinner party. Throw in a Caprese Salad and a warm serving of crusty bread, and you're golden.

DIRECTIONS

Heat 4 quarts of water in large stock pot until it begins to boil. Cook pasta according to package directions. Drain pasta, and set aside.

Preheat oven to 500 degrees (to broil).

While the pasta cooks, cut chicken into bite-size pieces, and set aside. Heat olive oil over medium heat in a sauté pan. When the oil is warm, add garlic and sauté for 2 minutes. Add sun-dried tomatoes, and sauté for another minute. Add chicken, and sauté until cooked through.

Place pine nuts on a dry baking sheet, and broil in oven until slightly toasted, or toast them in a dry saucepan. Keep a watchful eye as the pine nuts may brown quickly.

In a large bowl, combine crumbled feta, toasted pine nuts, and olives. Add the sautéed chicken mixture to the dry ingredients, and toss thoroughly.

Add drained pasta to the chicken mixture. Toss again, adding additional olive oil as needed. Salt and pepper to taste. Enjoy!

BREAD & DIPPING OIL

Heat a fresh round loaf of your favorite bread and slice evenly. In a dipping bowl, mix extra virgin olive oil and balsamic vinegar. Then top with freshly ground black pepper and salt. Finish off with a sprinkle of fresh Parmesan or Romano cheese.

Caprese Salad (serves 4-6)

INGREDIENTS:

4 vine-ripened tomatoes

8 ounces fresh mozzarella cheese (preferably, packaged in water)

Salt, to taste

8 fresh basil leaves

Freshly ground black pepper

Olive oil, to taste

Balsamic vinegar, to taste

One of my favorite summer treats is sitting down to a fresh Caprese Salad with tomato and basil straight from my garden.

DIRECTIONS

Slice tomatoes and fresh mozzarella. Spread tomato slices on platter, and sprinkle with salt. On top of tomato slices, layer fresh mozzarella and then a basil leaf, repeating this pattern until through with ingredients. After layering, sprinkle with pepper and drizzle with olive oil and balsamic vinegar. Serve at room temperature, making sure to be creative with your presentation.

THE LIES WE BELIEVE

Around the age of ten, while the other kids in my area were having fun and being normal, I began running a one-mile circular route through my neighborhood. I trained myself to run without stopping, keeping my times and building up my endurance. At age twelve, I joined the local track team. In high school, I ran as part of my regular basketball practices. By the time I entered college, running had become part of my regular exercise routine until I hit my thirties and decided it was too hard on my back, at which point I took up the competitive sport of strolling.

The bad news about this insignificant trivia is that I was never a good runner nor did I enjoy it. I have little endurance, and I'm pretty sure that God did not give me a single endorphin—I've yet to experience what perky joggers refer to as a "runner's high." These happy runners appear to have escaped the law of gravity, bouncing down the road like they're out for their morning jog on the moon. I really don't like these people.

Despite the fact that I was ill-fitted for running, I did appreciate the health benefits. The spiritual ones, too. Running outside gave me time to pray and consider what God was doing in my life. I remember an especially poignant illustration the Lord gave me during one of those afternoon jogs. I was about twenty minutes into my route when something on the sidewalk caught my eye. At first glance I thought I'd happened upon a deceased baby alligator, except that Nashville isn't a natural habitat for alligators, not even singer/songwriter ones. I then figured it must be a lizard of some sort, maybe someone's pet iguana or bearded dragon. I admit my reptile knowledge is limited.

Oddly enough, the most fascinating thing about this encounter was not determining the species of this creature but noting how it had met its most unfortunate death. Its head was stuck in a Dr. Pepper® can. I know this because I picked up the end of the can and the reptile's body hung limply from the opening. This, friends, is what we call a bad day.

Several theories about how a lizard could die in a soda can ran through my head while peering over him. My best guess was that he'd somehow escaped from his cage and begun to roam the city streets, motivated by wanderlust. While on his hot summer day's trek, he grew thirsty, spotted the Dr. Pepper logo, was lured in by the drops of glistening syrup, and decided to have himself a taste. But once he'd wedged his head through the mouth of the can, he couldn't back himself out. I could have furthered my investigation but decided to leave things as they were in case a bouncing runner came by.

The dead lizard incident happened during the initial writing of this study. It made me think of the times I'd discovered a few drops of seductive pleasure, a sip of intoxicating success, and thought I'd found life. I recalled the moments when I'd squeezed myself into something I was certain would bring respite from the heat but left me suffocating instead. How easy these places were to walk into but nearly impossible to back out of.

Our false gods are full of false promises but empty as crushed soda cans. They lure us in with lies and deception, never mentioning the costs attached to giving ourselves to them. This week, my hope is that we'll more clearly see through the lies, while pressing into the immutable promises and blessings of the one true God. One of my favorite things about the Lord, that sets Him apart from every one of our idols, is that He is light and there is no darkness in Him (1 John 1:5). He is the truth, and it's impossible for Him to lie. He does not lure; He leads. His paths do not end in suffocation; they give life. I can't wait to get started with you. I almost want to run there.

DAY ONE
BEHIND EVERY FALSE GOD IS A LIE

GENESIS 3:6a: The woman saw that the tree was good for food and delightful to look at, and that it was desirable for obtaining wisdom.

When I first wrote *No Other Gods* the interactive Internet was just crashing onto the scene. The dawn of social media had arrived and suddenly we could measure our successes and failures not only within our own communities but also against people across the globe. We quickly became more aware of what we didn't have and what others had on a grander scale. The idolatry that had been mostly accessible through television and magazines was now at our fingertips at all hours and in countless forms.

When I scroll through my social media feed and see the achievements and accolades of the people I follow, I can easily slip into the trap of thinking I need what they have for life and happiness. I can lose myself online, believing that if only I had children like my friends, or a kitchen like hers, or the money to look younger when I'm feeling bad about myself, or a husband who could take me on that extraordinary vacation, I would be happy.

The promises of today's false gods haven't really changed as much as they've become nearly impossible to get away from. But the way of freedom is not inaccessible, even as we use social media to serve, love, and stay in touch with those we're called to. We'll see this week that we need not be overcome as we pull back the curtain on our false gods by pulling back the cover of God's Word. If the Internet and social media have left you feeling discouraged or discontent or trapped in comparison thinking, the good news is that the truth still sets us free.

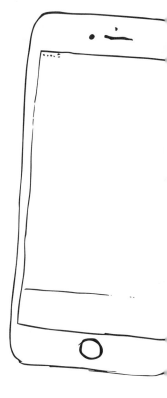

Today we'll focus on two small portions of Scripture that you're probably familiar with. Don't let familiarity keep you from their depth.

READ GENESIS 2:15-17 AND 3:1-6.

What blatant lie did Satan tell Eve that directly opposed what God told Adam in 2:17?

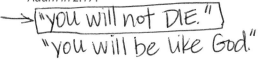
"you will not DIE."
"you will be like God."

SESSION FOUR: THE LIES WE BELIEVE   65

What three realities attracted Eve to the fruit (v. 6)? ②

① *good for food, delight to the eyes, and* ③ *desired to make one wise.*

Verse 6 is personal to me because I, like Eve, have talked myself into things that later brought much pain and regret. It's helpful to see how she got there.

First, Eve saw that the fruit of the tree was good for **food** .

READ GENESIS 1:29 AND 2:16-17.

Why is Eve's first reason for eating the fruit insufficient justification based on these verses?

Because God gave her plenty of other options for FOOD.

I can relate to Eve's second reason for eating the forbidden fruit—it was pleasing to the eye. After buying my first home I've become a helpless slave to visually pleasing environments. I can rarely afford to keep up with my eye, but color, textures, lighting, and art have stolen my affections. So I understand how something that was "delightful to look at" could propel Eve an inch closer to her infamous bite.

I also can't help but think of the marriages that have been wounded or destroyed because of an affair that began with someone who was pleasing to the eye. We don't have to stretch our imaginations to grasp that even though Eve existed in a beautiful environment and walked in unhindered intimacy with God, when an angelic devil whispered sweetly in her ear and that piece of fruit shimmered in the sun's glow, she reached for what would change the course of humanity forever.

PERSONAL TAKE: The media knows the power of "pleasing to the eye." What are some ways the media (including social media) try to appeal to what our eyes long to look at?

The last of the three convincing reasons that encouraged Eve to eat the fruit was that she believed it to be "desirable for obtaining wisdom" (3:6). The King James says, "to make one wise." Consider the Hebrew definition of the word translated as *wise*: "to be prudent, be circumspect, wisely understand, prosper."[1]

PERSONAL REFLECTION: Can you think of something that attracted you based on the wisdom or understanding you could gain from it?

school trainings

There is overlap in this exercise but, generally speaking, answer the following (Identify all that apply.):

1. *"Good for food" is primarily about meeting Eve's _____ needs.*
   Mental   Emotional   (Physical)   Spiritual

2. *"Pleasing to the eye" (NIV) is more about meeting her _____ needs.*
   Mental   (Emotional)   (Physical)   Spiritual

3. *"Desirable for obtaining wisdom" is about meeting her _____ needs.*
   (Mental)   Emotional   Physical   (Spiritual)

Eve perceived the fruit would offer satisfaction for an array of needs: mental, physical, emotional, and even arguably spiritual. Yet the fruit provided none of what she had hoped for and everything she would have desperately wanted to avoid.

READ GENESIS 3:7-8.

Adam and Eve would yet experience additional consequences for their choices. But what consequences did they experience in these verses?

- embarrasment / shame
- fear
- self-concious

PERSONAL REFLECTION: How does the process of Eve giving into temptation parallel your own vulnerability to being similarly deceived?

instant gratification
truth becomes "foggy", compromise becomes easy

God is the Creator of beauty and the Author of all that's pleasing to the eye. Still, He's more supreme than beauty and His word greater than all that is lovely to look upon. Eve's partaking of the fruit was not a sin because the fruit was beautiful but because the Lord had told her and Adam not to eat of it. In other words, we can't justify our sin simply because something is beautiful.

God is the Creator of beauty and the Author of all that's pleasing to the eye. Still, He's more supreme than beauty and His word greater than all that is lovely to look upon.

Recognizing the areas in which we're being deceived, and the consequences that follow, will give us an advantage in ridding our lives of our idols. Though the fruit hanging from the tree may look desirable to us, and may have the ability to briefly satisfy our cravings, recognizing the deception around anything that claims to bring us life other than God is half our battle.

 My prayer is that today the curtain was pulled back on the lies propping up your false gods, even the ones that appear beautiful. Christ's love for you and His desire for your freedom are more glorious than whatever is pleasing to your eye. May we learn from Eve's journey so we're not similarly deceived. The life that is truly life is waiting for you to take hold of it.

9-15-19

DAY TWO
BEHIND EVERY
FALSE GOD IS DECEIT

GENESIS 3:7a: Then the eyes of both of them were opened,
and they knew they were naked.

Exposing the lies behind our idols is fundamental to recognizing the thin props by which they're upheld. It's like pulling back the curtain on the Wizard of Oz. What once appeared all-powerful is nothing but a sham. Behind the veil we see the frailty, the meaningless levers being pulled, and the deceit.

From memory, list the three things that attracted Eve to the fruit from the tree of the knowledge of good and evil. (The answers are found in Genesis 3:6 if you need to review.)

T F
1. good for food ☑ ☐

T F
2. good to the eye/pleasurable ☑ ☐

T F
3. gaining "wisdom" ☑ ☑

I'd read this passage countless times before something struck me that I'd never seen before.

Look at the three reasons Eve ate the fruit, and identify the ones that proved true. (For example, was it true that the fruit was pleasing to the eye?) How many did you identify as true?

2. ③

I'm going to argue that all three proved true. Here's why: Evidently the tree was good for food because Adam and Eve ate the fruit and neither died of poisoning nor is there any mention of them getting sick. The fruit was pleasing to the eye, which is pretty straightforward—Eve saw it and was drawn to it.

That the fruit was desirable for gaining wisdom is a little more complicated, but read Genesis 3:4-5. What does Satan argue in these verses? (Fill in the blanks below.)

God knows that when you eat it your eyes will be ___opened___
and you will be like ___God___, *knowing good and evil.*

NOW READ GENESIS 3:7 AND 3:22.

According to these verses were Satan's statements true?

(Yes)   No   Somewhat True

Satan seems to have told Adam and Eve what was true. First, they didn't physically die. At least not in that moment. Second, their eyes were opened and they became like God in the sense that they now knew good and evil.

 Given that the knowledge of good and evil is a type of wisdom, would you feel comfortable circling "desirable for obtaining wisdom" as true about Eve's perception of the fruit?

(Yes)   (No)

God didn't want them to know that info...

But that "wisdom" drew them away from God...?

I've yet to discover any lies related to what Eve thought the fruit would do for her, which is intriguing to me (and initially perplexing).

LOOK AT 1 TIMOTHY 2:13-14.

What does verse 14 say about Eve before she sinned by eating of the tree?

She was "deceived"

PERSONAL RESPONSE: How has deception led you into sin in the past? How can you specifically guard against being deceived?

• You must know the TRUTH!
• Thinking the 'sin' will give you something you'd never have or making things more 'FUN'...

Michael Wells of Abiding Life Ministries made this profound statement: "Often the enemy uses facts to add to and augment his position. He will use true things, but he never uses them to lead a person to truth."[2] Let that sink in for a moment. If you're currently struggling with your finances, you might think something along the lines of, *I don't have enough money to pay my bills this month; I'm going to lose everything.* It might be true that you don't have enough money to pay your bills, but the truth is that God will take care of your every need (Matt. 6:25-30).

My boyfriend/husband has rejected me; I will never be loved. It might be true that you've been rejected or abandoned by someone you love, but it isn't the truth that you will never be loved again or aren't loved now. God will never forsake us or withdraw His love (Deut. 31:6).

I remember a situation in which I put forth my very best efforts in a work setting only to find out I wasn't chosen for a particular role I desperately wanted. It was true that several others had been chosen and I wasn't "what they were looking for." But the truth was that God would use that disappointment to lead me down a different path, one in which I'd still be using my gifts but in a different environment.

I'm sure you can see the pattern here. It's the same pattern we find in Genesis 3. Satan spoke a lot of true statements, yet none of them was the truth. This is where deception plays such a significant role in our lives. Though we've all succumbed to believing blatant lies, it's more common to be captivated by sheer deception.

PERSONAL TAKE: What do you think is the difference between a lie and deception?

deception takes on a more intentional, and manipulative nuance.

In Genesis 3:4 Satan told Eve, "No! You will not die." This turned out to be a blatant lie. It directly countered God's warning that they would die if they ate of the fruit of the tree of the knowledge of good and evil. Though their physical deaths came later, they died spiritually that day. From that point on in the conversation, Satan took the deceptive approach. He added to and twisted God's words to mislead Eve.

When reflecting on Genesis 3, I think it's important we note all that was lost on that day in addition to experiencing the consequence of spiritual death. Sin entered the world. We were moved from a perfect garden to a fractured earth. Our relationship with God was broken. We suddenly knew both good and evil—a knowledge I don't believe we were intended to carry, a form of wisdom never meant for us to have. Our eyes were opened in extremely harmful and painful ways (for example, suddenly Adam and Eve were aware of their nakedness). All the things Satan told Adam and Eve were true couldn't compare to what God told them was truth.

I know firsthand how difficult it is to turn away from what God has forbidden, especially when it appears to be beautiful and true. I've also experienced the profound love behind His commands, because His truth is always more glorious and fulfilling than what the world tells us is true.

His truth is always more glorious and fulfilling than what the world tells us is true.

PERSONAL REFLECTION: Write about a situation in which you are (or have been) trying to discern what is true from what is the truth. Keep in mind that circumstances often present things as "true," but God's Word always presents the truth.

It's true that no one has pursued me in a way I desire. But the truth is God loves me, I'm beautiful, and He has a plan for me, and I'm not unlovable.

Close this day by meditating on the truth of what God told Adam in Genesis 2:15-17. What were Adam and Eve free to do?

eat of every tree in the garden, except tree of knowledge of good & evil.

When we start to play with God's original words we can quickly become deceived by counterfeit philosophies. Once deceived we start focusing on the counterfeit, reading books and blogs that support what we want to believe. We align ourselves with people who champion what's false until we talk ourselves into twisting the fruit from the tree and biting into its lie. At that point we lose our freedom. If there's anything I want for you to experience as a result of this study, it's the unrivaled freedom that comes when Jesus is the ultimate desire of our hearts.

To stick with the truth we have to know it and choose it.

You've probably heard that those taught to recognize counterfeit money train by studying the original. Spending time scrutinizing a million possible counterfeits makes little sense when all you need to know is the real thing. Eve needed to dwell on what the Lord had declared about being free to eat from any tree, except that one. To stick with the truth, we have to know it and choose it.

Dear friend, my prayer for you today is that you will know God's word, because it is always truth and always for your freedom. The blessings He bestows and the peace of His presence will far surpass any glimmering god we may have our eye on. "For freedom Christ set us free. Stand firm then and don't submit again to a yoke of slavery" (Gal. 5:1).

My thoughts that arise, "yea, but can doing things God's way REALLY be as exciting/fun as another way?"
↳ Satan wants to twist God's awesome plan for my life by making me second-guess God's goodness

God told Adam/Eve they could eat from ANY tree in the garden.
What "tree" am I desiring? Is it the excluded one? Is it in his freedom?

What were the other trees like?
Did they look as good/pleasurable?
'Sinful' things look good/fun/exciting -
↳ But they're never fulfilling.

DAY THREE
BEHIND EVERY FALSE GOD IS INTIMIDATION

2 CHRONICLES 32:8a: He has only human strength, but we have the LORD our God to help us and to fight our battles.

Today we'll look at an Old Testament account of truth and lies colliding in front of the people of Jerusalem. It's one of the most clear-cut scriptural examples of both forces at work. As you commit to telling yourself the truths of God's Word, I hope you're encouraged by this account.

READ 2 CHRONICLES 31:20–32:23.

As you read, list the statements of truth and statements attacking the truth.

STATEMENTS OF TRUTH	STATEMENTS ATTACKING TRUTH
Be strong and courageous. Do not be dismayed ... but with us is the Lord, to help fight our battles	"Is not Hezekiah misleading you?" "Do you not know what my fathers and I have done to all the peoples?" "Who ..was able to deliver their lands from out of my hand" "So the God of Hezekiah will not deliver his ppl from my hand"

How would you summarize Sennacherib's tactics against the Israelites (32:10-19)?

Listing "evidence" of his strength to defeat. Questioning Hezekiah's confidence in God to scare him

One of Sennacherib's phrases in verse 10 caught my attention: "What are you relying on that you remain in Jerusalem under siege?" (The NIV says, "On what are you basing your confidence?") I can think of a few times when I chose to "remain under siege" because I believed that God wanted me right where I was. Perhaps it's been the same for you. It could be a troubling job, a difficult marriage, an ailing church, or a trying roommate situation. Regardless of the circumstances, believing that God will protect and take care of us in difficult situations requires confidence. Sennacherib's words attacked the root of that confidence by casting doubt on Hezekiah's leadership and the nature of God Himself. It reminds me a lot of Satan coming to Eve in the garden and asking, "Did God really say … ?" (Gen. 3:1).

PERSONAL REFLECTION: With which of Sennacherib's strategies can you most closely identify when you think of the ways the world or Satan tries to dissuade you from the truth?

- It hasn't happened before. Why would this time be any different?
↳ Making me question what I ask from God.

Cutting through the lies we encounter on a daily basis is like plodding through the jungle with a machete. It can be a moment-by-moment battle. We jump on social media and feel deflated when someone has something we're convinced would make us happy. We lose a job we'd staked our year on, and the first thought we're tempted to believe is, *God has forsaken me.* We read the mommy blogs and convince ourselves we're not measuring up. We scan the magazine covers and become discouraged at how far we fall short of the perfect image. Meanwhile, the rich promises and freeing truths found in Scripture collect dust on our side tables.

Cutting through the lies we encounter on a daily basis is like plodding through the jungle with a machete.

What truths did Hezekiah declare to the military officers about both God and Sennacherib in verses 32:7-8?

Be strong and courageous
Do not be dismayed
With us is the Lord our God to help fight

As a result of these truths what did he tell them to do and not to do (v. 7)?

Be strong / courageous
DO NOT FEAR!

How do John 16:33 and 1 John 4:4 amplify Hezekiah's words in 2 Chronicles?

God has already won — overcome!
There is nothing to fear.
God is WITH US!

PERSONAL REFLECTION: As you consider the challenges you face and the lies that can often accompany those challenges, how do these verses encourage you? Meditate on how these truths would affect your circumstances if you really believed them.

It would keep me from wanting to rely on physical/tangible things (friends, money)

Look at 2 Chronicles 31:20-21. What kind of king had Hezekiah been?

good, right, and faithful

Now look at verse 1 of chapter 32. What happened?

Sennacherib came and invaded and encamped around them!

PERSONAL TAKE: What does this tell you about obedient people who go through trials?

that we will go through them. Trials don't mean we've done something wrong

Be encouraged if you've been seeking God yet find yourself in a difficult season. Hezekiah had been faithful, and still he was attacked. We should take heart that Israel stood up to the threats and sieges of Sennacherib because they were able to identify the truth from the lies.

Today's study is essential to our journey. So much of our enslavement to modern-day idols begins with believing our enemies are big and our God is small. Hezekiah was convinced of two truths: His God was the LORD (Yahweh) and Sennacherib had only the strength of a human. Because he knew the truth he could call out the enemy's lie.

PERSONAL REFLECTION: What lie that you believe keeps one of your idols in business? Write down a truth from God's Word that combats this lie. After writing down that truth, ask the Lord to help you live in the light of its reality. He is the LORD our God who helps us "fight our battles" (2 Chron. 32:8).

No one really wants you → seeking after the attention of man/approval.

I need security in later life so I need lots of $ now to save → trust in MONEY.

*Read Psalm 107:9 * Jeremiah 2:12-13*

Matthew 6:33 / 1 Timothy 6:17,

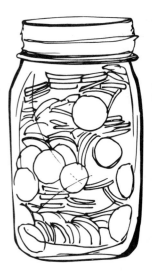

THE DOORS WE LEAVE OPEN

ROMANS 16:19b: I want you to be wise about what is good, and yet innocent about what is evil.

As I mentioned at the top of this week, one thing that has changed about the world in which we live since I first wrote *No Other Gods* is the advent of social media. No one could have anticipated how radically it has transformed our lives. I've spent some time pondering the difference between the amoral platform of social media and the moral and immoral content it transports. We don't need to shut the door on the platform itself but we do need to be vigilant about the content and images we allow entrance into our lives.

Our screens are wide-open doors for anyone and anything to infiltrate our thinking, desires, or beliefs without us even realizing it. Social media didn't invent the idols of our hearts, but it's done a bang-up job of exposing them.

READ 2 TIMOTHY 3:1-17.

It's important to note that the people Paul referred to were false teachers who had cropped up in Ephesus. Most troubling is that these individuals professed to be Christians. I wonder if Paul had Jesus' words in mind when he listed the harmful characteristics. In Matthew 7:15-20, Jesus taught that false prophets would be like ravenous wolves dressed in sheep's clothing. The way to tell their true nature is by their fruit. In 2 Timothy 3:2-5, Paul showed that despite the Christian claims of these false teachers, the fruit of their lives told a different story.

Verses 2-5 list nineteen characteristics of people who live for themselves as opposed to Christ living through them. They are:

1. lovers of self
2. lovers of money
3. boastful
4. proud
5. demeaning
6. disobedient to parents
7. ungrateful
8. unholy

9. unloving
10. irreconcilable
11. slanderers
12. without self-control
13. brutal
14. without love for what is good
15. traitors
16. reckless
17. conceited
18. lovers of pleasure rather than lovers of God
19. holding to the form of godliness but denying its power

Turn on a screen and we soon realize those characteristics were not isolated to people in the first century. They are as prevalent in these last days as they were in those last days.

Which of these negative characteristics do you encounter most often on social media, in movies, books, magazines, and blogs? List your top three.

1. Lovers of money.
2. Without self-control
3. Lovers of pleasure

With which of these do you personally struggle? List your top three. Were any the same as above?

1. Lover of money → to keep me secure.
2. Proud
3. Unloving

I want you to connect the dots here. We probably wouldn't nourish a relationship with someone who bears these negative characteristics. Yet we invite people of this nature into our homes through what we watch and read on our screens. Or we feast on sites that promote the idolatry that causes us to behave like the people we're watching or reading about. The things we read, watch, and listen to have a profound effect on us, yet we often justify them. Have you ever thought, like I have, *There's stuff I know I shouldn't watch in this show, but it has an overall good message. I appreciate the art form. This is counter to what I know Jesus teaches, but I'm mature enough to handle it. This is crude, but it's hilarious, and I need a good laugh. It doesn't bother my conscience. The good outweighs the bad. I just need something mindless.*

The things we read, watch, and listen to have a profound effect on us, yet we often justify them.

Those who know my writing know I'm not talking about separating ourselves in a way that precludes us from loving the world and being bearers of the gospel. This is about not allowing ourselves to be corrupted by the world.

PERSONAL TAKE: Why do you think verse 8 says that they resist the truth?

Because by resisting truth, they could allow themselves to do as they please.

Look back at verse 6, and answer the following three questions:

What specific place were some of the people described trying to get into?

Creep into households

What was their objective once inside?

Capture weak women,

How did these types of people enter a household? Name the specific word that is used.

CREEP!

PERSONAL REFLECTION: Why do you think they infiltrated in this way as opposed to coming through the front door in broad daylight?

If they did it in broad daylight, its easier to recognize the act, and to fight back. But "creeped" in is hiding, unknown.

When you consider the open doors of your household don't think of the physical entryways. Think about every screen you have in your home. Every book, smartphone, magazine, and pair of headphones. Whereas a deceiver once had to creep into a household, he can now parade in through our wide-open devices. Here's an exercise that might shed light on any doors (screens) you've left unguarded.

PERSONAL REFLECTION: Look up the following verses. What guidelines do these passages give for what you should and shouldn't dwell on? Be specific and make sure to focus on the positive sides as well as the negative.

Psalm 1:1-2 *don't walk among the wicked, sinful people*
meditate on God, his Word all day

Psalm 119:127-128 recognize God's word as TRUTH/Right
hate every false way.

Romans 16:17-19 notice who creates division/obstacles to TRUTH
they deceive others AVOID them

Philippians 4:8 Think on: truth, honorable, pure, just,
commendable, excellent, worthy of praise!

1 Thessalonians 4:3
avoid sexual immorality — control your own body —
don't divulge in passions

Every day we're exposed to the lies of our false gods in our culture and media. Here's the tricky part—the lies often appear friendly and attractive, thoughtful, and always innocuous. Many of them are so subtle we no longer detect them. And we dismiss the ones that are glaringly blatant as things we believe don't affect us. Most of us aren't out choosing friends who are slanderous, self-absorbed, abusive, conceited, and disrespectful. But perhaps these traits are creeping into our lives during prime time, in our secret moments on that one illicit site, at the movies, on our favorite blogs and social media feeds.

PERSONAL RESPONSE: Has the Lord convicted you today through His Word about anything you need to stop watching, reading, or interacting with online and instead replace it with time spent dwelling on what is good, virtuous, and true? If so, write about it in the space provided. Include a prayer of commitment to lay it aside.

I remember a friend telling me that she was convicted to give up a certain show. She was pained to even speak it aloud, flinching like she might not be able to live without its characters in her life. If you've been in the church any length of time you know what I'm talking about—we treat conviction like we just picked up the norovirus. But conviction is something to be embraced because it means the Holy Spirit is active in our lives. It's God speaking to us. And He will only convict us to stop doing something—or start doing something—because it's for our good. We may feel grief when parting with an idol we depend on or enjoy, but if true conviction is present, we'll begin to look at it as something that was taking the place of God, something that was controlling us. We won't have to look for loopholes because we'll be expectant for what God will do in this newly created space.

Conviction is something to be embraced because it means the Holy Spirit is active in our lives.

Tomorrow we're going to focus on the second half of 2 Timothy 3, which offers us the hope of God's Word. It will be a salve for whatever discomfort you might be experiencing today through the Holy Spirit's conviction. Hang on, and don't try to justify or look for excuses—the end result is being complete and equipped for all the good work God has for you (2 Tim. 3:17).

DAY FIVE
WE CAN ONLY
KNOW A LIE BY THE TRUTH

2 TIMOTHY 3:14a: But as for you, continue in what you have
learned and firmly believed.

My niece Harper and my nephew Will are learning the concept
of lying. If Harper gets a fact wrong, such as, "Hey Kelly, did
you know that two plus two is six." Will is quick to correct her,
"No Harper, it's four. Kelly, Harper's lying." We're still working
out the finer points here.

I tried to explain to Will that just because you say something that's not true
doesn't necessarily mean you're lying, albeit this was not an easy concept
to describe. Despite his early confusion, Will processed one piece correctly
without even realizing it—he determined what was false based on what he
knew was true.

We don't typically determine what's true based on what's a lie; rather
we determine lies based on truth. Taking yesterday's list of worldly
characteristics from 2 Timothy 3 as an example, how is it that we can know
being a lover of self is problematic? What's so wrong with being a lover of
money? Can't we love pleasure instead of God—what's the matter with
that? What about being proud, disobedient to authority, or ungrateful—
why not? We can only know that the characteristics we studied yesterday
are detrimental because of the truths revealed in Scripture. We'll focus on
this concept today.

*What were the false teachers described in yesterday's list resisting
(2 Tim. 3:8)?*

READ 2 TIMOTHY 3:10-17.

We've already determined that in order to identify a lie we must know the
truth. Jesus claimed in John 14:6 that He is the truth. Therefore, if we're to
navigate this world's vain philosophies, empty promises, and wounding
deceptions, we must be well acquainted with the revelation of Jesus and
His Word. This is precisely what Paul passed on to Timothy.

Write a brief explanation of how truth can be passed on in each of the following ways and why each way is significant.

❏ *Teaching*

❏ *Conduct*

❏ *Purpose*

❏ *Faith*

❏ *Patience*

❏ *Love*

❏ *Endurance*

❏ *Persecutions and sufferings*

PERSONAL TAKE: Why do you think Paul told Timothy to continue in what he'd learned (the truths of God's Word) immediately after talking about deceivers (vv. 13-15)?

How does this apply to us in our current culture?

On a recent flight, I grabbed a magazine out of the seat pocket and read an interview with a female celebrity. She described another actress whom she especially revered because that actress was living out "her truth" really well. I'm seeing and hearing this a lot these days—truth preceded by a pronoun—his truth, her truth, my truth, your truth.

In 2 Timothy 3:13-17, Paul didn't implore Timothy to be rooted in Paul's truth or even Timothy's own truth. In what did he encourage Timothy to be rooted?

Turn back to 2 Timothy 1:5,13. Who taught Timothy the Scriptures?

Many people center their lives on themselves and the philosophies of this world, but Paul has something altogether different in mind for those who are believers. "But as for you … ," he says (3:14). These tender words set us apart from following the lies of our culture. Paul encouraged Timothy to continue in what he'd learned and believed. The Greek word for *continue* is *menō*, which means *to abide, dwell, or remain*. Consider the significance of this word. We'd never say, "I'm so glad I had a chance to stop by and see you for five minutes. It was so nice to dwell and abide with you." Instead the nature of the word implies an ongoing process.

PERSONAL RESPONSE: In what ways can you specifically continue (dwell, abide, remain) in what you've learned from the Word of God? What activities, practices, or habits hinder your dwelling in what you've learned and believed? Give this some thought.

Whether you're like Timothy with a family legacy of faith (2 Tim. 1:5) and a great spiritual mentor (Paul), or you recently became a follower of Jesus, you're called to continue in the truths of the gospel.

PERSONAL TAKE: Based on today's passage, what case can you make for the effectiveness of being taught God's Word and spending time with people who teach it?

Second Timothy 3:16 reveals to us that Scripture comes from _____ and is profitable for what four things?

Verse 12 states that everyone who desires to live a godly life in Christ will suffer persecution. Often this will come at the hands of deceivers. Paul urged us to dwell in the Bible because it's so easy to jump ship when things get difficult—but this is precisely when we're to stay rooted in the hope of Scripture.

Look back at verse 16. The Scriptures are useful for teaching, rebuking, correcting, and training in _____?

Righteousness is the polar opposite of all nineteen self-centered characteristics we read about yesterday. As we learn to live righteously through God's truth (not my truth or your truth), we become equipped for every good work. Other words for *equipped* are *adequate, complete, competent*. As we close our week together, I'm inspired by the image of a woman who's capable of executing every good work the Lord has given her to do. My desire for you is that you'll be that kind of woman. We can futilely spend our time chasing false gods and being deceived by their lies, or we can dwell in the truth we've been taught from the Scriptures, being made ready for every good work the Lord created us to accomplish.

No worldly pleasure or promise can rival the joy and adventure of accomplishing the divine tasks God's given you to do.

In Colossians 1:10, Paul says he hasn't stopped praying for the Colossians, "so that [they] may walk worthy of the Lord, fully pleasing to him: bearing fruit in every good work." I don't want you to miss this fruit for anything in the world. No worldly pleasure or promise can rival the joy and adventure of accomplishing the divine tasks God's given you to do.

PERSONAL REFLECTION: What was your most significant takeaway from this week, and what are you going to do with it?

NOTES

SESSION FOUR VIEWER GUIDE

→ "half breeds" "scum" → known as this.

SAMARITAN WOMAN

John 4:6 Jesus is the <u>way</u>, the TRUTH, and the <u>life</u>!

John 4:7-10
- when we KNOW Jesus, everything we do is different.
- We seek/ask/pursue differently than the world.
- We seek better things/different questions by knowing TRUTH/JESUS.

John 4:11-12
- Jesus are you greater than what I am seeking after for a happy life (false gods)?? YES!
  → Samaritan: "Are you greater than Jacob?" (Jesus)

• The idea of our false gods is always greater than the reality of them.

John 4:13-18
- "Living water" = Holy Spirit (John 7:37-39)
- physical thirst vs. spiritual thirst. Jesus meets a much greater THIRST/need!
- Are we living out OUR truth or Gods TRUTH. Our truth is not good truth.

Jesus didn't accomodate or affirm her TRUTH.

① He meets her in her truth.

② Jesus redeems her from her truth.

③ He covered her w/ the truth of His Gospel.
Eph. 1:13

GROUP DISCUSSION

What one thing from this video teaching really resonated with you? Why?

Why is the idea of our false gods always better than the reality of them?

Why do we ask better questions and seek better gifts when we know who Jesus truly is?

How does knowing Jesus change what we want in life? Has that happened to you?

Kelly says, "Our truth is never a good reality." What does she mean? How has Jesus redeemed you from your truth?

What does it look like to worship in spirit and in truth?

The Samaritan woman told the townspeople that Jesus knew everything she'd ever done (even the bad things), and yet she seemed excited about that (John 4:29). Why was she able to be excited, and how does this encourage you as you consider Christ's love for you?

Lauri's White Turkey Chili (serves 6-8)

INGREDIENTS:	In the original *No Other Gods* study, I includ-
1 tablespoon olive oil	ed Lauri's Chili recipe made with beef. Ten
1 small yellow onion, chopped	years later, we're having to think more about
¼-½ cup jalapeño peppers, chopped	our health, so, of course, we're now making
2 tablespoons ground cumin	chili with ground turkey. I know, this sounds
2 tablespoons fresh sage, chopped	so boring. But, it's surprisingly tasty. Give this
Pinch of red pepper flakes	recipe a try, and whatever you do, just don't
Salt, to taste	mention it's turkey chili.
1 pound ground turkey	
2 (15-ounce) cans Cannellini or	
Great Northern Beans	

DIRECTIONS

In a stock pot, warm olive oil over medium-high heat. Add onion, jalapeño, spices, and salt. Add ground turkey, and brown. Next add beans and a bit more salt. Fill one empty can with water and pour into mixture. Bring to a boil, and simmer for 15-20 minutes. Add salt and spices to taste. Serve with cornbread and butter or tortilla chips and salsa!

When we expect things from people that they can't BE/DO, we set them up for failure and set us up for dissapointment.

→ *can They become our IDOLS. We want this person to meet our needs fully when they NEVER WILL.*

WHEN PEOPLE ARE OUR GODS

This week of study is the most personal to me. While I've made some idols out of material goods and pleasures, people have been the greatest source of idolatry for me. Putting someone on a pedestal isn't good for either party, by the way. Not for the person who's piling all her expectations and wants on another, nor for the one who's the recipient of all those impossible demands. When we look to people as the ultimate source to meet our needs and desires, everyone loses. Plus, it adds relationship drama. And exactly none of us are sitting around thinking, *if only I had just a little more drama in my life.*

The good news is that Jesus not only satisfies our hearts, He also puts our relationships in their proper places. I've found that when Jesus is my ultimate love, I'm able to love the people around me more wholly. When He is supreme, people become even more important to me, yet I don't excessively need them or demand things from them. I can't overstate how much change the Lord has brought about in my life in this area—my friends and family would be happy to fill you in. Still, we're never fully rid of our sin and struggles any more than you can peel an onion around once and think you've hit the core. Recently I had to shed another layer of that onion.

I was overwhelmed with work, and my Internet was down so I couldn't even swat at the things I was overwhelmed by. Plus, it was raining. If anyone is curious, a rainy day paired with the wrong circumstances is not a good combination for me. I was disappointed that no one was helping me! Couldn't people see I needed help? Hadn't all the smart people who love me weighed all the things I've done for them alongside all the things they've done for me and seen that they owe me? This was all so clear.

During my negative ruminating and despair, I happened to be making my way through Philippians 4:10-14. I ran straight into that well-known verse,

Philippians 4:13: "I can do all things through Christ who strengthens me" (NKJV). (The Bible always gets me when I'm in a mood.) I don't remember how old I was when I was first introduced to Philippians 4:13. Not very. I do remember the verse was spelled out on the classroom wall of my Christian elementary school in bubble letters made of construction paper. I remember memorizing it in AWANA (Christian kid throwback). I also remember thinking, *Huh. I wonder what exactly this verse means because there are all kinds of things I wish I had the strength for that I don't seem to have.*

I wanted to be a better athlete. I worked myself hard on the basketball court, but I finished my high school career only having accomplished some things, not all things. But I kind of already knew this verse wasn't about basketball. Even the times when I claimed this verse for spiritual purposes, I had strength for some things but not for all of them. Without minimizing the lengths to which Jesus' strength can go or the circumstances in which His strength can be expressed through us, it's helpful to understand the context of this verse.

It occurred to me in the middle of my disappointment with "everyone who wasn't helping me" that Paul could write about being able to do all things through Christ who strengthened him precisely in times when people couldn't fully meet his needs—even if they wanted to. We're not sure why the Philippians "lacked the opportunity" (Phil. 4:10) to demonstrate their care for Paul, but for whatever reason, he went without their support for a time.

When people don't meet your needs, can't meet your needs, or are called away to someone with greater needs at the moment, you can still do all the things Christ has called you to do because of His strength in you. Paul could write Philippians 4:13 whether he had all the best people encouraging him and helping him materially, or whether they were absent for a time. This is also why Paul's two statements, "I can do all things through Christ" and "I have learned the secret of being content" are so closely connected.

I'm continually learning that there are seasons when you're surrounded by the people you need, and the relationships with your family and friends are firing on all cylinders. But there are also seasons when, regardless of intent, the people from whom you often draw strength may not be able to give it to you. It's in these times of relational scarcity when we discover the true Source of our strength and contentment. When the rug of what people can give us is ripped out from underneath us, for whatever the reason, we learn how much of our fulfillment and joy springs from Christ. Take heart if you're in a time of scarcity. There's no better Source to draw from than Christ. He is the One who will supply all your needs from His infinite riches stored in the bottomless trove of His glory.

DAY ONE
WHAT WE'LL
DO FOR LOVE

GENESIS 29:31a: When the LORD saw that Leah was unloved,
he opened her womb.

Last week, we looked at the lies and deception that surround
our false gods. Like bees circling a sunflower, a false god can't
thrive without its orbiting lies. The person of Jesus quiets all
this swirling and buzzing with His clarifying words of truth—
not my truth or your truth, but His truth. It is with His truth that
we'll ask Him to lead us this week as we look at one of the most
powerful idols of all: people.

People can become our gods without us even realizing it. A healthy
friendship can become enmeshed when either person puts the other on a
pedestal. A marriage becomes strained when one spouse looks to the other
to fulfill all of his or her desires. As a married friend once told me, "The man
I married makes a wonderful husband," and after a nicely placed pause, "but
a terrible savior."

READ JAMES 4:1-3.

What causes struggles and fights among us?

> passions are at war w/us — we desire & do not
> have, covet & can't obtain

What do our unsanctified desires and passions do inside us?

> causes quarrels and fights
> & wage war inside of us.

Look at the beginning of verse 2. The CSB translation reads, "You desire and
do not have. You murder and covet and cannot obtain." The word *desire* (or
crave or *lust*) is taken from the Greek word *epithymeō*, which literally means
"to set the heart upon, i.e. long for (rightfully or otherwise)—covet, desire,
would fain, lust (after)."[1] This is key to more fully understanding what James
is saying.

*Based on this definition, are the cravings that often cause us pain or get
us into trouble necessarily desires for wrong or evil things?*
Yes   No

I used to read this passage in James convinced that my desires for sinful things were the only concern. It never occurred to me that my desires for good things, such as people, could also turn excessive and disproportionate, causing the pain and unrest that James describes. The story of Rachel and Leah depicts the trouble that comes when people become our gods better than any other I know. Their saga is deeply meaningful to me because I've struggled in many of the same ways.

There's more Scripture reading than normal today, but at least it's a story about someone else's drama—you should enjoy this. Be encouraged that we modern-day women didn't invent the lovely outcroppings of idolatry such as jealousy, manipulation, or competition. They've been around a year or two, or four thousand.

READ GENESIS 29:16-30.

Who did Jacob desire to marry?

Leah   (Rachel)   Both

How did Laban deceive Jacob? (Mark the correct answer.)

❏ *He gave Rachel to Jacob but doubled the work Jacob owed him.*
❏ *He gave Leah to Jacob and Rachel to Esau.*
☑ *He gave Leah (instead of Rachel) to Jacob, and then gave Rachel to Jacob in return for another seven years of work.*
❏ *He promised Rachel to Jacob and then sent him back to Canaan.*

PERSONAL TAKE: How did Laban's deception position Leah for a marriage full of heartache?

He made her vulnerable and set her w/ a man he knew he did not desire.

Now that you understand the context of how both Leah's and Rachel's marriages to Jacob began, let's enter their story.

READ GENESIS 29:31–30:21.

Genesis 29:30 says that Jacob loved Rachel ___more___ than Leah.

Genesis 29:31 plainly says that Leah was ___hated___ .

PERSONAL REFLECTION: Describe the last time you felt unloved by someone whom you deeply wanted to love you.

Some of you might have to go back to junior high to remember being rejected by a boyfriend or friend. Some might be in the middle of a painful marriage or a long season of singleness where you're experiencing the pain of not being loved or chosen. Others may have grown up with parents who didn't show them the love for which they longed. Though I don't know the depths of the rejections you've endured or are enduring, one truth for certain is revealed in this story.

How did God know that Leah was unloved (29:31)?

He ~~saw~~. saw

The God of the Bible is a seeing God. Whatever you're going through, He sees you. And not only is He a God who sees but one who enters into your pain by acting on your behalf.

Whatever you're going through, He sees you.

In what way did God act in Leah's life when He saw she was not loved?

He opened her womb— to allow her to conceive

What does each of the following names of Leah's children tell us about her longing for Jacob?

❏ *Reuben (29:32)* my husband will love me now.

❏ *Levi (29:34)* My husband will be attached to me

❏ *Zebulun (30:20)* My husband will honor me.

Instead of seeing the gift of her children as God's blessing in her life, Leah viewed them as a way to capture the heart of her husband. I can relate to this. Sometimes I've used God's blessings as ways to obtain the things I want instead of returning my affection to Him. I have often hoped that I could win the love of another person by what I could bring to the table. I've tried to accomplish significant things to secure affirmation and offered my time and resources for affection—whatever would win the love I longed for.

YOUR TAKE: What is the fundamental contradiction of trying to earn a person's love? Why do we try to do it anyhow?

Ultimately, no one will truly satisfy us. So we spend all this time / effort trying to prove ourselves — and will find that up to them alone — we will not be satisfied.

Love we have to earn is no love at all.

Love we have to earn is no love at all. For Leah, having children was a way of trying to gain love, honor, and acceptance from Jacob. But his love would have been conditional love at best. Leah's devastation was that despite her childbearing, Jacob's heart was taken with Rachel. No amount of children would change the fact that he didn't love Leah the way he loved Rachel.

Did you notice with the birth of each child how increasingly desperate Leah became for any amount of affection she could get from her husband? Notice the progression. With Reuben she hoped for love. With Levi she hoped for attachment. With Zebulun she merely hoped to be treated with some respect.

I should mention here that a woman's desire to be loved by her husband is altogether right and good. God designed marriage in such a way that a husband should love his wife like Christ loved the church. Our desire to be loved by our spouses, parents, family members, and friends is a natural longing God planted within us. But when that longing becomes all-consuming, eclipsing our love for God, clouding our view of His blessings, and leaving years of discontent and manipulation in its wake, we've most likely made a person into a god.

PERSONAL TAKE: Look back at Genesis 30:14-16. Reuben is now old enough to be harvesting from the fields. Given the amount of time that's passed since Leah first began to chase Jacob's love, why is this part of the story particularly sad?

Because now she resorts to "buying" his affection. It no longer happens on it's own.

PERSONAL REFLECTION: Ponder Leah's desperation for Jacob and the way it manifested itself. Describe the void in her life that would have brought her to this point.

You become so desperate, you reach for anything to get that feeling / attention, etc.

Did you notice that Leah didn't even wait for Jacob to get home? She flew out to the field to let him know that she had him for the night. Leah knew she wasn't loved in the way she longed to be; she knew she'd given Jacob everything she had, and it wasn't enough. She also knew that Rachel would always be chosen ahead of her. And still she ran out to meet him for just one night of something that might feel a little like love.

PERSONAL REFLECTION: Have you ever given yourself to someone for mere crumbs in return (or know someone who has)? Explain. It doesn't have to be sexual in nature or involve the opposite sex. It could be a friend, child, parent, or boss.

Yes - friends in college. Put in a lot of effort to be friends, and yet they were always looking for other people. I was never enough.

We read a lot of Scripture today, with perhaps some of it feeling very personal. We won't find much resolution to this story until later this week. But, in the meantime, allow the story to permeate your heart. Let Leah's circumstances draw out your own longings, and ask the Holy Spirit to reveal ⟶ *to have a husband* the vacuum of desperation that may reside inside you. The forever good news is that Jesus is far more fit to fill the empty places in your heart than even the best of our Jacobs. *amen!*

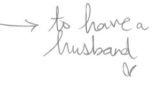

Psalm 146:5 says, "Happy is the one whose help is the God of Jacob, whose hope is in the LORD his God." When we scan the horizons of this earth, it's easy to set our hopes on a great many Jacobs. My desire is that we'll set our hopes on the God of Jacob instead. He's the only One able to satisfy our hearts' longings.

DAY TWO

WHEN WHAT YOU WANT ISN'T ENOUGH

JAMES 4:3: When you ask, you do not receive, because you ask with wrong motives, that you may spend what you get on your pleasures (NIV).

Yesterday, we focused our attention on Leah. Today, we'll look at Rachel. But before we go any further, I want to make sure you picked up on the moral of the story so far: those who have the love of a man are exceedingly happy, and those who don't are desperate and miserable.

I felt you could use some sarcasm today.

While we may not admit to buying into this concept, in our culture entire industries are built on this sentiment. Today we'll look at how "happy" Rachel was with the love of Jacob.

REREAD GENESIS 30:1-8.

Rachel told Jacob to give her sons or she would ___DIE___ .

Who was Rachel jealous of?

Leah - her sister

If Rachel had Jacob—which was everything Leah was convinced would make her happy—why was Rachel jealous of Leah?

Because she was having kids.

PERSONAL TAKE: Why do you think Jacob's love wasn't enough to satisfy Rachel?

She was comparing herself to another woman.

Though Rachel had everything that Leah wanted—the love of Jacob— you can argue that the reason Rachel was still miserable was because she couldn't bear children. We might think to ourselves, *If only that longing could have been fulfilled, she'd have been complete and satisfied having both husband and children.* Tuck that thought away. We'll come back to it.

PERSONAL REFLECTION: Look back at the emotions that surrounded Rachel's conversation with Jacob, as well as her response to each child her maidservant bore. What do you think it was like to be around Rachel at that time in her life?

moody/emotional walking on egg shells
turbulent   miserable

Notice the desperation that Rachel showed by settling for a child through her maidservant.

How was this similar to Leah settling for a night with Jacob?

Both very desperate

Both women were trying to control their circumstances. Both were willing to settle for crumbs. Both appear chronically unhappy. We're often so desperate for what we want that we'll do just about anything to get whatever feels mildly close.

→ and it ends up not being anything close to what we truly want ...

You've probably known women who were willing to sleep with someone just to be held, just to feel like someone desired them if only for a moment. Or maybe you don't just know that woman, but you are that woman. My utmost prayer is that through this study you'll be filled with the love of Jesus and discover an incomparably more fulfilling way to live. These are not Christian platitudes; Jesus Himself said that He came to bring life that's abundant (John 10:10). We experience this abundance when we follow Him in obedience.

CONTINUE THE STORY BY READING GENESIS 30:22-23.

Complete Rachel's statement: "God has taken away my

~~REPROACH~~."

Leah was not loved. Rachel had lived in disgrace. Both believed their answers lay with someone other than God. In other words, they'd both made people into false gods.

Who was Leah's?

Jacob— a husband

Who was Rachel's?

her children

The difference between the two was that Rachel finally got everything she wanted. God opened her womb, and she gave birth to Joseph. Rachel had the exclusive love of her husband, and now she had the son she'd always longed for. Though we don't get many more details about the rest of her life, this next passage is telling.

TURN AHEAD AND READ GENESIS 31:32-35.

What did Rachel steal?

household gods

Our theory that people satisfy us and make us happy isn't holding up well. Apparently being loved and having children wasn't enough for Rachel. Her striking beauty hadn't done it either (Gen. 29:17). She had it all, and yet on her way out of town, we find her stuffing false gods into her suitcase. Ones that weren't even hers.

PERSONAL REFLECTION:

1. Write about something/someone you don't have but are convinced would make you happy if you could obtain it.

a husband
more money/less debt
more friends

2. Describe a time when you finally got the very thing/person you longed for and it didn't make you as happy as you thought it would.

I have yet to get the thing mentioned above. But I understand that even when I do, my heart will still cont. searching...

The somewhat sad account of Leah's and Rachel's lives ends abruptly, and there's hardly another word written about them. I remember asking God what the lesson was in this story. Leah was homely and unloved and seemingly miserable; Rachel was beautiful and loved and finally birthed children, yet was cramming idols into her bag for her journey. *God, what's the treasure here? What's the takeaway?* I couldn't see it.

THIS. →

While not every story in the Bible has a moral or point, I sensed the Lord telling me, this is the lesson: It doesn't matter if you have it all and get everything your heart desires or if you're left wanting and unloved, neither is fulfilling. The two women had vastly different circumstances yet both were left hungry. Why? Because God was not the ultimate desire of their lives. Good things like husbands and children and social status had become the ultimate things, and in the end, they proved unable to satisfy. In fact, so much so that Rachel was found grasping for gods near the end of her life.

How often I've thought that if God would just give me most of what I hope for, then I'd really draw close to Him. This wasn't the case with Rachel, and it's not typically the case with us. Today, I want you to recognize that only God Himself can satiate your longings. Nothing compares to knowing Him and being His.

Only God Himself can satiate your longings. Nothing compares to knowing Him and being His.

You may be experiencing some uncomfortable moments as you look at how you've put people on pedestals and perhaps made them into saviors. But I promise this will be a freeing journey if you give Jesus His rightful place in your life. I've found that the more central He is to me, the more my relationships become rightly ordered. The more I look to Christ to meet my deepest needs, the less I expect people to be my saviors. There is none like Him.

Yes!!

They also no longer become central to my WORTH. Jesus does!

DAY THREE
FREE OF JEALOUSY AND STRIFE

EPHESIANS 2:4-5a: But God, who is rich in mercy, because of his great love that he had for us, made us alive with Christ.

When writing a Bible study, I'm always thankful that the Holy Spirit knows what you need to hear (1 John 2:27). I'm sure the Lord has spoken to you in ways I've never thought of or mentioned anywhere in this study. Hold fast to those treasures—they'll prove so meaningful to you.

Today I want us to look at how we can determine if we struggle with turning people into gods. Pastor Tim Keller said, "Idolatry is attached to everything. ... All your bitterness, all your impurity, all of your malice, all of our problems, everything that troubles us is a result of idolatry. And what is idolatry? *It's taking a good thing and making it an ultimate thing*" (emphasis mine).[2]

PERSONAL TAKE:

> *Reflect on the last two days of study. How did Leah make Jacob into an ultimate thing?*

She thought he held the power to give her what she wanted / ultimately to make her "happy" → put all her time into

> *How did Rachel make having children into an ultimate thing?* obtaining that.

She was holding that as a ~~symbol of her worth~~ + provoking others ~~to jealousy~~ when others didn't have it.

> *Look back to Day One of this week, and find the definition of the Greek word for* desire, *epithymeō (p. 91). Write it in the space provided.*

"TO SET THE HEART UPON; LONG FOR- COVET, DESIRE, WOULD FAIN, LUST."

We don't have to crave evil things for an idol to be in the making. Like Leah's desire for Jacob to love her and Rachel's desire for children, often our desires are for inherently good things. But even these desires cause heartache and devastation when they're excessive. When they become more important to us than God, they rule us.

PERSONAL REFLECTION: Has the definition of *epithymeō* reframed the way you think about the desires that battle within you? Describe.

My Desires:
- *marriage*
- *family*
- *LMFT*
- *friends/ community*

*It makes it easier to identify.
- are they taking my attention away from God? No...?*

As I mentioned on Day One of this week, for much of my life I was convinced that my idolatry problems were a result of my desires for sinful things. It never occurred to me that my desires for good things could also become overpowering and disproportionate, causing the pain and unrest that James described.

Look again at James 4:1-2, and record the detrimental list that results from unrestrained epithymeō. /passions at war within you.

-murder -fight
-covet -quarrel

With this list in mind, turn back to our story in Genesis 29:16–30:24. Leah and Rachel had warring desires within them that resulted in much of what James mentioned. In the exercise below, describe the specific instances where the characteristics I've listed for you played out in each person's life. (Some will show up more clearly in one or the other.) I've given you an example.

	LEAH	RACHEL
JEALOUSY		Leah was pregnant, she envied her (Gen. 30:1)
STRIFE/FIGHTING		
ANGER		• "Forcing" Jacob to give her children (30:1)
MANIPULATION	Leah bargaining for Jacob with the mandrake plants	• Giving Bilhah to Jacob to have children another way (Gen 30:3)
CONTROL	Giving her servant to Jacob when she could no longer bear children.	
UNFORGIVENESS	"Would you also take away my husband?"	

One way to tell if you have false gods, or have turned people into gods is the presence of strong or uncontrollable reactions and emotions. This story is fraught with them.

PERSONAL REFLECTION: Which of the listed sinful reactions do you struggle with the most? What unsanctified desire is at the root of your struggle? In the past I have so often struggled w/ JEALOUSY — always wishing I could be someone else/be funnier/prettier — all stemming from this DESIRE to be liked/loved by other people. IDOL

When we look to God instead of demanding people fix our circumstances or make us happy, we'll know peace.

of others like I did in the past.

Here are some questions that will help you discover if idolatry is at the root of your overwhelming emotions or reactions: When you're jealous of another person, what does he or she have that you're convinced you need for happiness? When you're consumed with anger, what is being threatened that you're certain you need or deserve? If you're constantly manipulating and controlling the situations around you, what is it that you're trying to protect? If you're harboring unforgiveness and bitterness, what was taken from you that you can't live without?

Can you see how all of these unruly emotions point toward a false god of some sort? We attempt to tame these emotions by calling a friend to vent, letting off steam at the gym, or shoving them below the surface. But not until we allow God to treat us at the place of our idolatry will we see our jealousy, anger, manipulation, unforgiveness, and bitterness lose their power. When we look to Him, instead of demanding people fix our circumstances or make us happy, we'll know a peace that Rachel and Leah struggled to find.

LOOK AT GENESIS 30:1-3.

When Rachel realized she wasn't having children, what was her feeling toward Leah (v. 1)?

Envied her.

What phrase in Genesis 30:1 shows how jealousy (or envy) can lead us to irrational thoughts and actions?

"Give me children or I shall DIE"
Put so much expectation/power onto having a CHILD.

PERSONAL TAKE: How do you see jealousy, manipulation, arrogance, strife, and so forth playing out on social media? Name some practical ways that you can refuse to contribute to this unhealthy swirl.

There is "picture-perfect-ness" everywhere/constant consumption of products.
– Limiting time on it / Blocking toxic ppl that trigger you

I want to highlight jealousy since it's such a prevalent indicator of false gods. Notice Rachel's costly words to Jacob on the heels of envying her sister's ability to bear children: "Give me sons, or I will die!" Also notice the element of panic attached to her jealousy, as if she had to remedy the situation immediately by whatever means necessary. A jealous rage can lead to regretful words and irrational actions.

As Rachel's jealousy billowed, she made an unreasonable request of Jacob. How did her out-of-control behavior cause him to respond (v. 2)?

With ANGER.

What was Rachel's solution to her problem (vv. 3-4)?

She gave him her servant - to control the situation — and have children by her.

Didn't trust God. Chose another route for her desire

Oftentimes our jealousy leads us to foolishly and inadequately attempt to remedy our situation. For Rachel, her overpowering desire for children caused her to be jealous of Leah. Her jealousy motivated her to demand from Jacob something that was out of his control. Her inability to get what she wanted prompted her to say something she surely didn't mean—that she'd rather die if she couldn't have children. Her out-of-control desires—for something good, we must remember—led her to try to remedy the situation on her own, which ultimately wouldn't do for her what she'd hoped. (We'll understand this more fully in tomorrow's study.)

People will do almost anything when something threatens their ultimate thing. God so patiently delivered me from this type of entanglement. My freedom didn't come as a result of God giving me everything I wanted and was jealous for—I know you're surprised. Rather it came in discovering that everything I truly longed for was found in Jesus and His provision for me. God's words in Scripture absolutely brought healing and transformation to me and will do the same for you. His words will meet you where you are, and your story of deliverance will be uniquely yours.

His words will meet you where you are, and your story of deliverance will be uniquely yours.

One passage that meant a lot to me during my time of deliverance was Ephesians 2:1-10. Meditate on these verses, and look for any keys to freedom from the consequences of idolatry. List your findings.

God's grace

We used to be people who were "carrying out the inclinations of our flesh and thoughts" (Eph. 2:3). This was before our old nature was put to death with Christ when we believed in Him as our Savior. While a spiritual battle is still active within us, we're no longer controlled by our cravings and lusts. We're no longer bound to jealousy and revenge and bitterness when we don't get what we want, when we are mistreated, or when we experience loss. Why? Because Jesus Christ is our ultimate prize, and the far lesser things that vie for our attention are nothing compared to who He is and what He can do for us.

amen!

We don't always feel as though our sinful nature has been crucified, nor do we always feel raised up and alive in Christ, as Paul stated in Ephesians 2. But these are true realities for those who know Christ as Savior. As believers, I encourage you to claim the truths of Scripture even when you don't feel them. No matter your wounds or unmet longings, you don't have to live like Rachel and Leah who so often succumbed to striving and defeat.

End today in prayer by reading Ephesians 2:1-10 aloud, and agree with God about what He says is true of you.

DAY FOUR
WHEN WE SEE GOD

GENESIS 30:23b: God has taken away my disgrace.

I'm wondering if certain thoughts have crossed your mind during the course of this study like, *What's wrong with having a few things I'm a little too dependent on? Everyone has one or two excessive attachments in their lives.* It's easy to justify revolving our world around a few obsessions that are good things by nature, much like Rachel and Leah did. But often the "good" desires, even ministry, can cause just as much chaos and unrest in our lives as the wrong ones.

Regardless of how detestable or presentable our false gods are, they edge God out to the perimeters of our hearts. And this is the great tragedy: missing God in our lives because we haven't left Him any room. We glance at Him for a moment, thanking Him for this gift or that, and then run on to the next idol. I don't want you to miss God like Rachel and Leah did—like I did for a time. God was at work in their lives but they couldn't see it. They were too busy chasing the people they thought would fulfill them. Today we'll look at an instance in each of their lives in which they turned their hearts to the Lord. Unfortunately they had a hard time staying there.

REREAD GENESIS 29:31-35.

LEAH

Not only did God see that Leah was unloved, He did something specific for her. Remind yourself of what God did (Gen. 29:31).

PERSONAL TAKE: Why do you think God opened Leah's womb in response to her being unloved?

As a reminder that He sees her

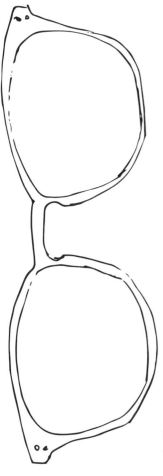

When Leah gave birth to Judah, Genesis 29:35 says that she:

❏ *Suffered depression*
❏ *Went to show Rachel*
☑ *Praised the Lord*
❏ *Danced*

PERSONAL TAKE: What did Leah stop doing after she had Judah, and why do you think this was significant?

She ceased bearing. She finally turned her atten to the Lord and not to her husband or she finally found fulfillment in the Lord

NOW REREAD GENESIS 30:1-9.

What made Leah realize that she had stopped having children, and what did she do as a result?

After trying to garner the affection of Jacob with her first three children, Leah finally turned her attention to the Lord, praising Him after she had Judah. She realized that her children weren't simply a means of capturing Jacob's love but were blessings given to her by God. He had seen her suffering and was active in her life. Then she stopped. Stopped having children, yes, but what she really stopped was the tiring chase for Jacob's love. Leah's praising God was an act of surrender that led to subsequent peace and rest. It was only when Rachel's maidservants started having children that Leah decided she needed to jump on the treadmill again.

What can you learn from Leah's story?

When we're looking @ someone/something else we will constantly be CHASING, STRUGGLING to get what we desire — but God changes all of that and TRULY satisfies.

RACHEL

REREAD GENESIS 30:22-23.

Verse 22 says that God remembered Rachel and listened to her. (Remember, this doesn't mean He'd forgotten her. Rather it was an indication that He was going to act on her behalf.) What does God having listened to Rachel imply she'd done?

When Rachel gave birth to Joseph, who did she say had taken away her disgrace? (Circle the correct answer below.)

Jacob   Joseph   Herself   (God)

After Rachel's successful scheme for her maidservant to bear her children, she claimed that God had given her a son and that she'd fought with her sister and won. In other words, she'd tried to take away her own disgrace and in a sense claimed success—"I've won."

PERSONAL TAKE: According to Genesis 30:23, Rachel had still felt the disgrace of barrenness (something that was amplified in her day) even after her maidservant bore Jacob a child. Why was God the only One who could take this disgrace away?

God is the only one who can change physical issues like bearing a child.

PERSONAL REFLECTION: From cover to cover the Bible reveals that only God can take away our disgrace, namely through His Son, Jesus. In what ways do you try to take away your own disgrace (shame or embarrassment)? How can you tell the difference between when you're trying to remove it and when God is?

It's always temporary
Can feel isolating if you're keeping something hidden

What can you learn from Rachel's story?

Even when all feels hopeless, God is aware of it and can act on your behalf.

Like Rachel and Leah, you may be looking to the false god of a person for fulfillment. Whether it's a husband, children, grandchildren, a boyfriend, or a friend, a human was never meant to take the place of God in your life. Leah's chase for love kept her from finding rest, and Rachel's barrenness kept her striving to take away her own disgrace.

A human was never meant to take the place of God in your life.

Read the following verses, noting how Christ meets these deep needs of our hearts. Write a brief explanation next to each passage.

Matthew 11:28-30
God can give us rest spiritually/physically

Romans 8:1 We are free from the effects (shame) of sin bc Jesus has taken it from us. We are not condemned.

Romans 8:31-32, 35-39
Nothing can separate us from God. God is FOR us.

Ephesians 3:16-19
We can be strengthened through Christ, we can find fullness in Him.

PERSONAL RESPONSE: Like Leah praised the Lord, take some time to praise Him for something He's done in your life. And like Rachel credited God for taking away her disgrace, thank Him for the ways His Son, Jesus, has delivered you from shame.

• So many things!
 – family
 – health
 – education
 – job (dream!)
 – car/home

Jesus has delivered me from insecurities that once gripped me. I feel set apart and am grateful for my life experiences. I'm grateful for the woman He's made me to be! ♡

Jesus is the satisfier of your soul. He's your peace and hope. He's the Shepherd who leads you. He's the One who tells you that you no longer have to strive, the One who takes away your disgrace. Set your gaze on Him instead of pinning your hopes on a person to fulfill you. Our Savior is calling those who are tired of the chase and weary of the fight to draw near.

Jesus is the satisfier of your soul.

9/27/19

DAY FIVE

WE LOVE BEST WHEN WE LOVE GOD MOST

JAMES 4:6b: God resists the proud but gives grace to the humble.

I'm cheering you on as you finish a challenging week. Contending with your idols is not for the faint of heart. Just the fact that you're more than halfway through this study tells me you're putting up a solid fight. I know you probably don't feel like a strong fighter. I remember when the Lord came in for a full-on sweep of my heart, knocking my biggest idols off their pedestals. I desperately wanted victory over them while I simultaneously tried to piece them back together, shard by shard—we're nothing if not at odds with ourselves. Some moments I felt like I was winning, while during others freedom seemed an impossible dream. What I didn't realize is that with every precious step of obedience God was severing a cord of bondage. When I failed to walk in obedience, I repented and God was compassionate and faithful to forgive me. He continued to lead me to freedom.

I remember during grad school years, losing this desire to be married. I had wanted to, but then felt it would never happen or feel like I was trapped. The desire was gone for some time. Just in the last year has God given me that desire again. Maybe @ that time I was making an idol of it/placing my worth on it. God taught me even if you are alone/unmarried, you can still find contentment in Him!

So if you have a fight going on, take heart, you're on the right track. The late pastor J. C. Ryle wrote, "A true Christian is one who has not only peace of conscience, but war within. He may be known by his warfare, as well as by his peace."[3] When we're simply coasting in life, it's unlikely we're warring against our flesh.

LET'S GO BACK TO OUR PASSAGE IN JAMES. READ JAMES 4:1-5.

What does James call the believers in Jesus who are "friends with the world"? This phrase is referring to the world's system, the things that are contrary to God, including His truth and His love. (Circle the correct answer.)

Pagans *Adulterous* *Rebellious* *Sinners*

Based on verse 5, why do you think he uses this specific language?

We're cheating on God for worthless things. Turned our love away from Him.

This passage is strong, no way around it. Thinking of myself as an adulteress in my morning quiet time isn't my favorite. And yet without watering anything down, if I look at it in the appropriate light, I can see the warning as affectionately loving. The only people who can be adulterous are those who are married. In essence, James is saying, "Remember, you're married to Christ!" This is what the apostle Paul taught when he referred to us, the church, as the bride of Christ. We are in union with Him. He is our provider, the lover of our souls, and our actual life. When we esteem the world's treasures as our functional gods, it is as if we are being unfaithful to our bridegroom Christ. We are looking for our desires to be met elsewhere. This idolatry is at the root of our jealousy, which is what causes our fighting and quarrels and wars.

Why do we feel like God doesn't satisfy? What am I/could I be doing wrong/not doing that makes me believe that?

PERSONAL TAKE: Read Exodus 20:4-5. What's the connection between our idols and God's jealousy? How does God's righteous jealousy for us show His love for us?

God's jealous for us and wants to see our affection towards Him - not other things!

I, the LORD your God, am a jealous God.
Exodus 20:5b

Its also in our best interest!

James 4:5 is a difficult verse for scholars to translate. The way I interpret it stems from its connection to verse 4 and what you just read in Exodus 20. I believe the Holy Spirit inside us is passionate for the things of the Lord. When we bow down to things like materialism, sexual immorality, people we think can meet our needs, our bank accounts, and the fleeting pleasures this world calls "life," well then, praise God, we have His very Spirit living inside us saying, *Enough! You're mine. You're the bride of Christ, and I'm jealous for you.*

PERSONAL REFLECTION: You may have heard it said that God is not jealous of us but for us. I believe this to be true. How have you seen God display His divine jealousy for you?

Constant pursual of me showering me w/ His TRUTH keeping me from bad things.

I do see it as a POSITIVE thing

If it's difficult for you to picture God's jealousy in a positive light, think of it this way. I have a friend whose son is in college. He's plunged headlong into many of the worldly pleasures and belief systems young adults are tempted by at this stage in life. He's left his friends in the church and is barely speaking to his family. He's drawing deep lines in the sand. He knows he can't live soundly in both places, so he's chosen sinful pleasures over abiding peace and godly community—God and gods can't coexist. My friend is jealous for her son and righteously grieved. She's passionate for his life and is petitioning God for him. It would be tragic if she were passive, not the least bit concerned. If that were the case, jealousy for him would be absent.

We saw from Rachel and Leah's story the tumult and unrest that comes when we live for people instead of for God. If this week you've been convicted of making a person into an idol, today I want to walk you through James 4:6-10. The Lord is righteously jealous for your affection.

READ JAMES 4:6-10.

PERSONAL REFLECTION AND RESPONSE: Take some time to sit before the Lord and walk through the exhortations found in these verses. Journal any thoughts you may have under each one.

1. **Submit to God.** Simply place yourself under His authority and control. He is a good Father, altogether true, compassionate, and kind. Is there any area of your life that you haven't placed under His care and control?

2. **Resist the devil, and draw near to God.** If you're believing any lies of the enemy or have allowed him ground in your life through disobedience, resist him and his ways by turning to God and His truth. Then, draw close to God by spending time in His presence, meditating on His Word, and praying as you have opportunity in your day.

3. **Cleanse your hands, and purify your heart.** Essentially this calls for repentance. Confess your sins, ask for forgiveness, and commit to living differently—God's way.

4. **Mourn your sin.** Our disobedience, such as putting people in the place of Christ, should cause us sadness and grief. This is a good thing (Eccl. 7:2). Share your grief with the Lord.

5. **Humble yourself before Christ, and rejoice that you're forgiven.** Rejoice that He will lift you up and restore you.

The desire to be loved and chosen is innate within us. This is a good and God-given desire. However, we've probably all been on both sides of what happens when this desire becomes the dominating force in a person's life. I've seen friendships and marriages destroyed over an obsessive and consuming desire to be loved.

I have a college friend who got married right after graduation. She captured the heart of the most exceptionally attractive, athletic, smart, and spiritual guy any of us knew. The two of them went on to have beautiful children. I remember thinking my friend had the perfect life. Years later, I was shocked to hear that their marriage was struggling, nearly to the point of divorce.

While not the only problem, my friend's insecurity and her desperate desire to be loved in a way that no human can possibly provide was the major catalyst behind her crumbling marriage. She kept abnormal tabs on her husband, questioned him relentlessly, and obsessively tried to control his every move.

When I think of my friend in light of the passage in James, she exemplifies a good desire gone astray. Her good desire for her husband to love her became obsessive and all-consuming. At the very root, her husband had become her idol, her god, her savior. Neither person could sustain this.

I praise the Lord that He redeemed that marriage. Both people submitted to Christ and began the journey of setting their affections on Him first. This was not a quick or tidy process, but their testimony is profound. They both love Jesus more than ever before, and as a result of that priority, they now love each other more than either thought possible.

James 4:6 says that God gives grace to the humble. If you long to be free of the idolatry of people, it all begins with His grace. Humble yourself, dear one, and be certain that He will lift you up.

SESSION FIVE VIEWER GUIDE

Though Jacob would never choose you, I CHOOSE you. God did something greater than making Jacob love her!

RACHEL AND LEAH

Gen 29 is not FAR from the beginning of CREATION — the ♡ universe, tides, sun/moon, **AND** God SAW one ♡ unloved woman! What does this say about our GOD!?!!!? Why didn't God solve Leah's problem? By making Jacob LOVE her?? Instead he opened her womb... Why?

w/her sons: (God invited her into the genealogy of Jesus!) Leah had the son JUDAH. setting?? ...

maybe He'll (love) me
maybe he'll be (attached) to me
maybe he'll treat me w/ honor/respect
(6th son later).

Our false gods will only make us DROP OUR EXPECTATIONS!

V. 35
" This time I will praise the Lord...
then stopped bearing children. " → She ceased her striving. Found PEACE!

Leah thinks Rachel is the luckiest! youngest most beautiful has has stolen the ♡ of Jacob. BUT is she really?? happy...

GROUP DISCUSSION

What one thing from this video teaching really resonated with you? Why?

Why are we so prone to make people into idols? How has that happened in your life?

Do you see yourself in either Rachel or Leah? If so, how?

What are some of the consequences of setting people up on the "god pedestal"? Which of these have you experienced?

If Rachel and Leah had trusted God's heart and plan for their lives, would their relationships with Jacob and their attitudes about having children have changed? How would your life change if you totally trusted God's heart and plan for you?

What safeguards can we establish to help us not make people into idols or gods?

• Good desires can be bad when they become ULTIMATE things / govern us.

Read 30:C As soon as Rachel begins bearing children, Leah wants back in the competition. Uses her slave to have kids.

we're desperate for anything that will feel like LOVE. even for just one night...

Video sessions available for purchase or rent at LIFEWAY.COM/NOOTHERGODS

Milk Chocolate, White Chocolate, and Toffee Chip Cookies (Yields 60)

INGREDIENTS:

2 cups butter, softened	2 cups white chocolate chips
2 cups granulated sugar	2 cups semi-sweet chocolate chips
2 cups packed brown sugar	½-1 cup toffee bits, available for purchase in baking aisle
4 large eggs	Cooking spray
2 teaspoons vanilla	
5 cups quick-cooking oats	
4 cups all-purpose flour	
1 teaspoon salt	
2 teaspoons baking soda	
2 teaspoons baking powder	

DIRECTIONS

Preheat oven to 350 degrees.

In a large bowl, cream butter, granulated sugar, and brown sugar with a mixer at medium speed until light and fluffy. Add eggs and vanilla, stirring just until blended. In a food processor or blender, pulse oats until they reach the consistency of a fine powder. In a separate bowl, combine oats, flour, salt, baking soda, and baking powder. Stir until blended. Add dry mixture to the butter mixture 1 cup at a time, beating after every addition until blended. Stir in white chocolate chips, semi-sweet chocolate chips, and toffee bits.

Roll dough into 1-inch balls, and place 2 inches apart on a lightly greased cookie sheet.

Bake for 8-10 minutes or until lightly browned. Cool on the cookie sheet for 3 minutes. Then, remove cookies from the baking sheet, and cool completely on wire racks.

Every one of us needs at least one friend who can make a cookie. I don't know what it is about people who know how to make cookies, but a novice like myself can follow the instructions flawlessly and still end up with cookies that are too mushy, too dry, too gooey in the middle. But a cookie-making expert never fails in these ways. So pass this recipe off to someone who knows what she's doing. (This recipe makes a lot, so you can half it or freeze the dough you don't use and save it for a rainy day. When you're ready to break it out, just make sure to take the dough out of the freezer an hour before baking.)

Rachel: "Give me children or I will die"

Later on in Chp. 35 - Rachel died giving BIRTH. Almost as if (on 2nd child) God was telling her back then, "NO, if I gave you children, you will die". It's God's GRACE her womb was closed!

SESSION SIX

WHAT KEEPS YOU FROM SAYING GOODBYE

I usually think of the word *goodbye* in the sad terms of having to part with people I love and enjoy. I savor deep relationships and I'm not keen on turnover, so the whole concept of goodbye runs contrary to my nature. Of course, saying goodbye isn't such a bad thing when we're parting with someone we're happy to see go. I remember an old pastor joke: "There are those in the church you're supposed to help out, and those you're supposed to help *out*." (This is not a godly joke, I know.) I suppose the pain or joy of a goodbye is totally dependent on whom or what we're saying goodbye to. Sometimes goodbyes are heartbreaking, other times joyful.

Alas, bittersweet goodbyes make matters more complicated. Bidding farewell to the false gods with which we struggle most tends to fall into this category. On one hand, we want to rid them from our lives because we know they hinder our relationships with Jesus. On the other hand, they often bring us pleasure, security, and familiarity no matter how temporary or costly. The thought of parting with them ushers in grief, even fear. Not all goodbyes are cut and dried.

I once had an especially unhealthy relationship that just about killed me to release. It was dead in the water. It bore no fruit. It brought the Lord no pleasure. It saddled me with misery. Still, there were things I would miss about it. Anyone else ever been this dysfunctionally conflicted? I knew I had to cut ties for my spiritual health and general sanity, but I still grieved over the loss for many months. Somewhere in the middle of all that dramatic mourning—because I can be dramatic—I came across a portion of the prophet Samuel's story that revitalized me.

The people of Israel had rejected God as their King, having pined for what everyone else had—a human king who sat on a tangible throne. God granted Israel's request and appointed Samuel to anoint Saul as king. Samuel poured a flask of oil over Saul's head, kissed him, and their journey and friendship began. Down the road Saul's heart rebelled against the Lord. He spared the best of the Amalekite's cattle for an offering even though the Lord had commanded him to destroy the whole lot (1 Sam. 15). Saul's version of sacrifice became more important to him than God's definition of obedience. To obey is always better than sacrifice (1 Sam. 15:22). As a result of Saul's rebellion, God rejected him as king over Israel.

And Samuel mourned.

After a while, the Lord said to Samuel, "How long are you going to mourn for Saul, since I have rejected him as king over Israel? Fill your horn with oil and go. I am sending you to Jesse of Bethlehem because I have selected a king from his sons" (1 Sam. 16:1). Israel had pinned its hopes and dreams on King Saul, but God had turned to another man to lead His people. And though Samuel was a righteous man, he had trouble moving on.

And sometimes, so do we. I don't have too many horns lying around, but the words, "fill your horn with oil and go" awakened me from a miserable slumber. Time to find a horn and some oil and get on with it; the Holy Spirit's conviction was clear. Wallowing in my woe-is-me mentality was causing me to miss out on the warm and welcoming sounds of new hellos. I was still grieving a past goodbye while new relationships and opportunities lay ahead.

For Samuel, God had a new king for him to anoint, and Samuel couldn't do this while lamenting the old one. A shepherd boy was unwittingly waiting in the fields for Samuel to relinquish what had been so Samuel could participate in what was to be. King David was part of Samuel's future, but Samuel couldn't have gotten there while still mourning Saul. No sense in spending the precious present mourning for the past when God has already moved on.

What new thing is the Lord asking of you? Is there anything old or cold you're still giving your thoughts, emotions, or energies to? Do you need to say goodbye to something in the past so you can embrace the present? How long, dear one, will you mourn? Fill your horn with oil. Be on your way. The Lord is doing a new thing.

DAY ONE
ROSE-COLORED MEMORIES

DEUTERONOMY 8:16: He gave you manna to
eat in the wilderness, something your ancestors
had never known, to humble and test you
so that in the end it might go well with you (NIV).

Minhas queridas—that's Portuguese for "my dear ones." I'm taking Portuguese classes right now and feel I need to show progress. Please be excited for me. Oh wait, but this is about you, *minhas queridas*. I'm so excited for you, so encouraged to see you taking your idols to task to make room for the living God. Your reward is a life of bearing fruit, which means a life of purpose and impact and joy. Even better, you're gaining a greater measure of the presence of Jesus Christ and deeper intimacy with Him. No idol—whether possession, career, pleasure, or person—comes close to that.

Over the past few weeks we've looked at false gods both from a broad perspective and an uncomfortably personal one. If your persistent thought has been, *so-and-so would really benefit from this study,* well, then it might be time to ask the Holy Spirit to do some work in your own heart. He's good at showing us our dependence on false gods we might not be aware of. After giving Him freedom to work in you, then you can pass the study on to that dear friend who's got a ton of false gods cluttering her life. Although maybe you shouldn't tell her that.

So far in our study, we've been defining our false gods, naming them, praying against them, and repenting of them. This week we'll look at leaving them. As a sentimental soul who doesn't love change, I'm not especially fond of goodbyes. However, I've found that some partings are the only path to new hellos.

READ NUMBERS 11:1-17.

The Israelites who'd been miraculously freed from Egypt aren't looking so good here. They had two major complaints. Complete these statements:

They were sick of eating __manna__.

They were craving __meat__.

LOL!

I really don't know what the Israelites' problem was—to eat bread all day and have it be God-ordained? I'm totally lost. I'm thinking their manna wasn't exactly what I have in mind. Still.

READ EXODUS 16:31.

Describe what the manna was like.

coriander seed tasted like a wafer made
white w/ HONEY.

Look at Deuteronomy 8:3,16. According to these verses, what makes you think that manna might have been a no-frills type of food?

"to humble you"
"man does not live on bread alone"

To what "end" was God using this humbling and testing?

to test their hearts ♡ ?
so they can rely on God ... & not food.

Though God was using the manna to humble and test them, I'm grateful for the promise at the end of verse 16. That "in the end it might go well with you" (NIV), or "cause you to prosper" (CSB). Or from the translation I grew up on, "to do thee good at thy latter end" (KJV). Times of vast desert spaces where I'm living on less than the bare minimum are not my favorite seasons. I call it less than the bare minimum because the Lord said He didn't want the Israelites to live on bread alone, and manna was less than that.

Seasons of trials can be seen as good things (Deut. 8:16)

PERSONAL REFLECTION: Describe a time when you went through a season of leanness that later proved beneficial?

College - no close friends - God met w/ me on a personal level. Told me that God is all I need.

The manna the Israelites were living on wasn't quite enough. It didn't fully suffice. The Lord put them in this position so they would learn the richness of depending on Him instead of on themselves, their provisions, or their false gods. He also wanted to do them good in the end. This is the "making room" part of the study. Do you believe that God wants to do you good in the spaces that your false gods are currently inhabiting? Do you believe He wants to prosper you? Too often we associate the idea of turning from our false gods with a life of misery and legalism, when in reality it means we've created more room for God to do good in our lives. Someone give me an amen.

Too often we associate the idea of turning from our false gods with a life of misery and legalism, when in reality it means we've created more room for God to do good in our lives.

PERSONAL RESPONSE: If you're going through a time of leanness in your relationships, whether it's related to your finances, health, job, or even a spiritual matter, write a prayer to the Lord dedicating this season to Him. Tell Him that you want this time in your life to serve a greater purpose—one where you come to know Him more deeply and where He works a surprising good for a later time.

I first wrote this study during a season that was lean on many fronts. I was emotionally depleted. I lost a group of my closest friends because we were walking in different directions. My career wasn't bringing in enough ✳ income. I told a friend how tired I was of struggling so hard for a living. Then I amended my statement—"actually a little less than a living." She was amused by my qualification and could afford to be—she wrote hit country songs for a living.

At any rate, for several years I really did make slightly less than a living. Yet somehow I was always provided for. Whatever I lacked because I couldn't provide for myself, God filled with a sweet measure of provision unique to me and my desires. God often uses scarcity in our lives to draw us to dependency on Himself.

What word in Numbers 11:4 is used to describe the Israelites' desire for meat?

(Crave)　　　　　Need　　　　　Hope

Needing and wanting are one thing, craving (or lusting) implies something a bit more controlling in nature. Last week we learned that even good things can become false gods. These good things become a problem when they dictate our attitudes and actions or when we obsess over them. The Israelites cried out for foods such as fish and cucumbers and leeks. (Who knew the power of a leek?) There's nothing wrong with these foods, but the craving, crying, whining, and demanding was problematic.

Think of a false god that falls into the category of something inherently good. How is wanting or needing it different than craving it?

When we are CRAVING something, we'll do just about anything to get it, or justify the reasons to get it, or lower standards just to get it... It's controlling and feels like a strong pull/desire!

Looking back at Numbers 11:5, list the things the Israelites remembered about Egypt.

fish
cucumbers　　garlic
melons
leeks
onions

This next question not only fascinates me but also opens a window into how I tend to remember my own times of entangled living. According to the Israelites' memories, how much did they have to pay for all this (v. 5)?

cost nothing .

The NIV says that the Israelites remembered all this food as having "no cost." As you read Exodus 1:11-15 and 2:23-25, keep "no cost" in mind.

How in the world could they say all those years in Egypt cost them nothing? The Israelites were slaves in Egypt for more than four hundred years. The Egyptians killed their baby boys. They were forced into hard labor. Their taskmasters doubled their workload, and the Israelites groaned before God. Were the fish, the melons, the onions, and the garlic really at no cost?

PERSONAL TAKE: Why do you think the Israelites seemed to remember Egypt so fondly?

IDK →

They were freed but still in the desert — BEFORE the promise.

I remember when God moved me, rather forcefully, from a situation that had held me captive. The environment was miserable, and I was angst-ridden during the day and through the night, except for a few electrifying snippets of happiness that had no footing in holiness. Many months after God delivered me, I began to remember the whole ordeal through rose-colored lenses. I conveniently forgot all the pain and angst that was associated with that time in my life. I remembered only the "leeks" from that season. I forgot the disproportionate price I paid for them. I recalculated them as being free when really they cost me considerable parts of my life.

Perhaps you've said goodbye to some personal idols but are currently missing them because you're nourishing false memories. You've colored them rose. Close by asking God to give you clarity about that time in your life. Thank Him for bringing you into a new season.

PERSONAL RESPONSE: If you've said goodbye to a false god yet are still hanging onto that idol in your heart, write a prayer of relinquishment.

DAY TWO

TOO MUCH OF A GOOD THING

PSALM 106:15: He gave them their request;
but sent leanness into their soul (KJV).

It was a life-changing discovery to realize I was looking back at a terrible time in my life as somehow desirable. I was freed from undue grief and sadness over things that didn't need to be mourned because those times really weren't that great, after all. I wouldn't go back to those old places for anything —not even for every leek in the world.

I haven't always said goodbye to the things I should have. Too often, I've bid adieu externally while my heart remained attached. I think this is where the Israelites were—somewhere between Egypt and the promised land, between full-on captivity and full-on freedom. Welcome to the perils of the desert, that grand stretch of fiery sand that purges us from where we've been, preparing us for where we're going. Today we'll look at the Israelites' demands on God and the consequences of their unwillingness to say goodbye in their hearts.

Hard for me too since I attach to people/things easily...

**PICKING UP WHERE WE STOPPED YESTERDAY,
READ NUMBERS 11:18-35.**

PERSONAL TAKE: Why do you think the Lord gave them what they craved?

*He wanted them to recognize that what they *THOUGHT* they wanted, they will eventually not want.*

It's odd to think of God granting a request borne out of sin. But He wasn't capitulating to their demand. He gave them so much meat that it was nostril-filling and nauseating—a punishment for their rebellion. God didn't just fulfill their request, He overfilled it. What they'd so desperately wanted would become loathsome to them.

PERSONAL REFLECTION: Has the Lord ever given you something you kept demanding, even though it wasn't a good thing? If so, explain.

To avoid this, when I pray for something, I ask God "only if it is your will" and "in your timing"

These are the kinds of prayers we don't want answered.

READ PSALM 106:7-15.

Here we get another writer's perspective on what happened when the Israelites demanded meat from God in the desert.

The Israelites' craving for meat was intensified not only by their glorified memories of Egypt but also by their forgetfulness of God's provision. What were some of God's works they'd forgotten about?

abundance of God's love (v.7)
drying the Red Sea (v.9)
delivered them from foes (v.10)

Isn't it interesting that they remembered how good the garlic was but failed to remember the Red Sea drying up? That coming-out-of-Egypt thing was great, but man, those leeks! (My goal is to see how many times I can include the word *leeks* in this study.)

Look specifically at verse 15. Fill in the remainder of the phrase. God gave them what they asked for, but ...

"sent a wasting disease among them"

The KJV says, "He gave them their request; but sent leanness into their soul." I wonder if that's where they felt the real loss—in their souls? I remember my dad referencing this verse often in his messages and speaking this line with a certain cadence. To do it justice you need to read the phrase again and hold out the "ea" in "leanness"—really drag it out. Thank you, I needed you to have that experience.

Look up the word lean *or* leanness *in the dictionary, and note its definition. (Not in the context of leaning against something.)*

Lean (leanness): ~~be in or move into a stopping position~~
~~incline~~
~~deviation from perpendicular~~

"thin"
"no fat"
"efficient w/ no waste"

PERSONAL REFLECTION: Do you consistently battle (or have you battled) against a specific craving?

What might fulfilling that craving do to your soul, if its fulfillment is not a part of God's will?

always leaves you wanting more.

The unsanctified longings of our hearts are filled with irony. When the Lord finally gave the Israelites' what they wanted, He gave them so much that they were left with very little. Physically they were fat, but their souls were anemic. An understanding of this truth is foundational to us saying goodbye to our life of idolatry. We deceive ourselves when we think our gods will bring us anything but leanness of soul. In the Israelites' case, God provided the minimalist diet of manna so that their souls could feast on the Lord. Remember, He didn't want them to live by bread alone (Deut. 8:3). Instead, they craved the richness of quail while their souls starved. You could say that God gave them bread for their bodies so they could have meat for their souls. Instead, they demanded meat for their bodies which resulted in leanness of their souls.

READ DEUTERONOMY 8:1-20.

What good purposes might a season of leanness serve? List as many as you can find.

- humble us
- test our hearts
- To rely on God/words

Over the past few years I've struggled with the very temptations listed in Deuteronomy 8—believing I've achieved my own success, forgetting how the Lord led me through desert stretches, struggling with pride, thinking I somehow delivered myself from the strongholds that so gripped me. As I sit with this passage I never want to lose sight of the truth that anything good in my life is because of God and His goodness. He has delivered me. He has blessed me. It's all been Him. As I consider the places in my life that are still cavernous, I'm reminded that my fulfillment can come in one of two ways— my way that brings leanness or His way that will go well with me in the end.

He has delivered me. He has blessed me. It's all been Him.

Dear friend, I want you to trust the Lord with your cravings. Tell Him all about them, but ask Him to fill them in His way so that it may go well with you. So very, very well.

PERSONAL RESPONSE: Tell the Lord about the empty places in your life. Give Him your hunger and longings, asking Him to satisfy you in His way and His perfect time. Write your prayer below.

DAY THREE
FRUIT AND GIANTS

NUMBERS 13:30: Caleb stilled the people before
Moses, and said, Let us go up at once, and possess it;
for we are well able to overcome it (KJV).

During the aftermath of Hurricane Katrina, I saw a man being interviewed on television from the front stoop of his home in New Orleans. He was one of the few who stayed and stayed and kept staying. Even after his city had been ravaged, his home had flooded, drinking water was no longer available, and bodies were lying in the streets. When they asked why he remained, he said he couldn't think of a better place they could take him than where he was. He couldn't say goodbye to his home because he couldn't envision anything better.

We must trust that what God has for us will be better than what we're clinging to, even if we can't imagine it.

That image continues to remind me of the faith it takes to leave our false gods behind. We must trust that what God has for us will be better than what we're clinging to, even if we can't imagine it. The man from New Orleans could only envision what he'd known. Even as his world deteriorated around him, he still preferred the familiar over the unknown—even if the unknown promised better.

Today we find the Israelites in a similar situation. They didn't want to leave the desert for the promised land.

READ NUMBERS 13:1-33.

What specific aspects of the land did Moses want the twelve explorers to survey? List every detail you can find (vv. 17-20).

what the land is
if people are strong or weak
if people are few or many
if land is good/bad
if there are camps or
strongholds

What did Moses ask them to bring back (v. 20)? Circle the correct answer.
❏ *The king captured alive*
❏ *An idol from the land*
❏ *Dirt from the soil*
☒ *Fruit*

Why did he ask them to bring that?

To see if they were courageous?

Moses could have asked the spies to bring back a number of other things: currency, a brick from the wall, a piece of art, or a precious metal. But fruit from the land provides such rich imagery. A cluster of grapes in season speaks of abundance.

Fruit is metaphorically used throughout Scripture. Jesus tells us in the New Testament that we can recognize false prophets (and consequently true followers) by the fruit they yield (Matt. 7:15-20). Our lives are to bear fruit (John 15:5,16). God blesses us with the fruit of His Spirit (Gal. 5:22-23). Righteousness yields fruit (Prov. 11:30). We'll actually spend the last week of our study looking at the fruit God has appointed us to bear.

PERSONAL REFLECTION: Have you ever tasted or brought back fruit from a future promise? In other words, have you experienced a glimpse of the place or work that God would be calling you to in the future? Describe your experience and how that glimpse gave you the faith to keep pressing on. Here are some examples to jump-start your thinking: You visited a foreign country and knew you would one day adopt a child from that place. You led a small group Bible study and sensed you'd one day be in full-time ministry. You took a college class that you loved, and you knew God was calling you to a career in that field.

Speaking in front of others / leading a group → gave me hope / encouragement that I have a desire to teach / lead in future.

Numbers 13:2 (NIV) says, "Send some men to explore the land of Canaan, which I am ___GIVING___ to the Israelites."

PERSONAL TAKE: If the Lord was giving the land to the Israelites, why not have them just go in and take it? Why do you think He wanted them to explore it first?

> But the people who live there are powerful, and the cities are fortified and very large. We even saw descendants of Anak there.
> Numbers 13:28, NIV

God knows our strong ties to the familiar, even if it's the wilderness or a flooded house. I wonder if He wanted them to see glimpses of the land so they would be more apt to go in. I wonder if seeing just a bit of the blessing would serve as motivation for them to finally pick up and leave, as well as fuel for the fight that lay ahead.

Looking only at verse 27, what was the spies' initial report?

Flows with milk and honey

Read verse 28 in the margin. What small but powerful word starts the sentence?

" BUT "

That infamous word *but*—the three letter word upon which many a blessing has been lost. Oh the land flowed with milk and honey, but. The grapes were exploding, but. One cluster was so big two men had to carry it on a pole, but. Out of the fertile soil shot pomegranate and fig trees, but.

The people occupying the land were exceedingly large and much stronger than the Israelites, at least from the spies' perspective. The cities were large and fortified. Both the glorious and terrifying parts of the report were true. But they'd forgotten one big but. But God would go with them.

PERSONAL REFLECTION: What *but* is keeping you from leaving the old behind and walking in new obedience?

"but I won't be that good"
"but they won't like me"

Today's passage reveals an important spiritual truth: God's promises aren't necessarily realized without struggle. Just because He's promised you something doesn't mean you won't have to fight for it. Occasionally the Holy Spirit will show me a promise in God's Word that I'm absolutely convinced is for me in that moment. But soon after seeing the promise, circumstances that either appear contradictory to the promise or at least opposed to it often follow. I might have held and even tasted the promised fruit, but then, those giants and brick walls.

PERSONAL REFLECTION: What obstacles are you currently experiencing in your pursuit of God's promises?

READ NUMBERS 14:1-9.

What did Caleb and Joshua want to do after they saw the land? What did the rest of the Israelites want to do after hearing the full report?

They wanted to go in and go to the land. The Israelites wanted to go back to Egypt.

PERSONAL TAKE: What was the difference between Caleb and Joshua's perspective and the rest of the spies'? How are the obstacles in front of you clouding your vision of God's promises and His call for your obedience?

Joshua and Caleb saw the same things the other explorers had seen. Everyone was in agreement about what they'd witnessed. There was no dispute over the size of the people or the strength of their cities. The remarkable difference had to do with Joshua and Caleb's faith. Though they encountered the same strong people and high walls, they believed God's promise—He would give them the land.

Are the giants in your life keeping you from trusting God while pushing you to old familiar idols? Or are you holding to the promise He's given you, having faith that He can conquer your strongest opposition? If you're anything like me, it might be a little of both.

Under each respective column, list the "promises and fruit" you want to obtain, along with the associated "giants and walls" that stand in your way.

PROMISES AND FRUIT	GIANTS AND WALLS

Whatever you do, don't let a but keep you from the promise.

PERSONAL RESPONSE: Joshua and Caleb had faith in God's promises despite the obstacles, and they expressed that faith by believing God and ultimately obeying His command. In closing, ask the Lord to give you the faith you need to follow Him in obedience. Whatever you do, don't let a *but* keep you from the promise.

WHEN JESUS LOVES YOU

MARK 10:21a: Jesus looked at him and loved him (NIV).

You may have already gathered that I'm an avid fan of the Old Testament. I'm drawn to stories brimming with people I can relate to—people who encountered God in a broken and sinful world, setting their sights on the promises ahead. The people of the Old Testament were limited in their scope though, longing to look into the things we now understand since the coming of Jesus Christ.

I once heard an Old Testament scholar say that if the New Testament is the building, the Old Testament is the blueprint to that building. Meaning, you need to understand the architect's drawings to best understand the building's purpose and design. We've been learning a lot about that design, the relationship that the one true God desires to have with His people. Now, we'll see how this relationship came to us in the person of Jesus Christ.

Keeping in mind what we've gathered from our study of the Israelites, today let's move to the New Testament. To get us thinking on topic, I've included a journal entry from Alli, one of the original NOGS, that was included in the initial study.

> I have a hard time with change. I moved to Nashville five years ago from a medium-sized town in Iowa and have just in the last year been able to use the words "I love" in the same sentence as "Nashville." It wasn't that I didn't like the city, but it was that I was here in body and in Iowa in spirit.
>
> The other day I came across a pile of giveaways and saw two plastic juice glasses from my grandmother and a faded plastic Northern Iowa mug. I've tried to give these things away before but couldn't bring myself to do it because it felt like I was giving up a part of my Iowa past, a part of me. All of these little physical things I've been holding onto were little metaphors of the way my heart was grabbing anything that represented home for me. Not that there's anything wrong with holding onto

memorabilia, heirlooms, or things from my past. It's just that all the while I was praying that God would give me deep relationships here—would give me a home here—I felt like He was ignoring that prayer.

I realize now that He was just waiting for me to make room in my heart for exactly that. I'm finding that when I dwell on a memory or a tradition in unhealthy doses, it occupies parts of my brain that could otherwise be taking in my surroundings and what God may be trying to reveal to me. There is a place for sentimentality, but I've been a junkie, and living in the moment is a much fuller way to live.

Embracing the new often means parting with the things of the past. That's our week in a nutshell and the theme of today's study.

READ MARK 10:17-22. *(You can find this same account in Matthew 19:16-30 and Luke 18:18-30.)*

Why did this young man approach Christ?

He wanted to inherit eternal life

Do you think he was sincere? How does Scripture shed light on this question?

yes He called Jesus "good", and went away sorrowful...

Why did he walk away sad?

Because in his heart, he wasn't ready to give up his possessions-/money.

Jesus' response didn't mean that keeping the Ten Commandments and giving all you have to the poor will get you into heaven. Good works can't save a person. On the contrary, Jesus is demonstrating how impossible it is to earn one's salvation by keeping the law. While the young ruler may have thought that he'd kept the letter of the law since he was a child, Jesus revealed that the condition of his heart was of far greater importance. This young ruler had all the right religious boxes checked, but a false god was on the throne of his heart.

What was his false god?

$ money $

Look at verse 21 (NIV). Complete the sentence: "Jesus looked at him and
__loved__ *him."*

Right after Jesus looked at the man, what did He say to him?

"you lack one thing, go and sell all you have / give to the poor."

When people look at me with love in their hearts, I usually expect a compliment, an invitation to dinner, or at the very least a hug. Is anyone else surprised that Jesus instead followed up His look of love by telling the man what he lacked? That he needed to sell everything he had and give to the poor?

Jesus is grieved when He sees us give our lives to anything other than Him.

It's been my experience that when I tell someone I love them, it's best to not follow it up with, "Oh, and by the way, let's talk about what is glaringly absent from your life. And then perhaps we can spend a little time on how materialistic you are and how little you give to others." (I've tried this, and we can talk later about how that worked out.) Yet when Jesus confronts us it's always out of the deep love He has for us. He longs to release us from the bondage of what rules our hearts. He's grieved when He sees us give our lives to anything other than Him.

YOUR TAKE: In verse 19, Jesus mentioned five of the Ten Commandments; I've highlighted them below. What do these five commandments have in common that make them different from the first four?

1. *Do not have any other god before God.*
2. *Do not make an idol for yourself.*
3. *Do not take the Lord's name in vain.*
4. *Remember the Sabbath Day and keep it holy.*
5. Honor your Mother and Father.
6. Do not murder.
7. Do not commit adultery.
8. Do not steal.
9. Do not testify falsely against your neighbor.
10. *Do not covet.*

dealing w/ other humans.

In Matthew's Gospel we find that Jesus also included, "Love your neighbor as yourself" (19:19), which is recorded in Leviticus 19:18.

Which of the Ten Commandments, not spoken by Jesus, had the young ruler failed to keep? Give this some thought.

2. Do not make an idol for yourself
1. Do not have any gods before me

Jesus left out the commandments that had to do with a person's direct relationship with God and included the ones that dealt with a person's relationship to others (except for "do not covet"). When Jesus added that the young man needed to sell all He had and give to the poor, He revealed a few things: 1. God's commands need to take root in our hearts—it's possible to keep the commands on how we treat others, while still maintaining a self-centered heart. 2. Anything can be an idol in our hearts, thus breaking the first commandment. In this case it was the man's wealth. 3. No person, in his or her own power, can live up to the perfection God demands.

CONTINUE READING IN MARK 10, VERSES 23-31.

What is impossible with man but possible with God?

Salvation!

PERSONAL REFLECTION: What is most encouraging to you from this story of Jesus and the rich young ruler?

Jesus' heart - tender, sweet - towards the man - and to us as well - when we drift. He longs for us to come home. He's not angry / runs from us.

Jesus told the young man that he was lacking something, and to remedy that lack he had to give something up—in essence, he had to lack more. But the rich young ruler found it impossible to part with all of his stuff, so he walked away sorrowful. However, he didn't have to. He missed the saving reality that the One who asks us to lay down our false gods is the One who empowers us to do it. What's impossible to us is possible with Him.

You can't follow Jesus while your heart and trust are tied up elsewhere.

PERSONAL RESPONSE: What are you holding onto that you don't think you can part with? What step of obedience do you need to take while asking God to do the impossible?

Many of us imagine God ruling us with an iron fist, telling us everything we need to give up so we can measure up. This account tells a different story, beginning with the revelation that Jesus loved the rich young ruler. This young man would never be able to truly follow Jesus if money remained his god. You can't follow Jesus while your heart and trust are tied up elsewhere.

Where will we experience the rewards of following Jesus wholeheartedly (vv. 29-30)? (Circle the best answer.)

(Heaven)   (Earth)   Both   Neither

If the Lord is convicting you about a false god that's ruling your life, He's doing so from a heart bursting with love. He doesn't want you to miss the adventure of following Him for the stuff of this world. It's stuff that won't

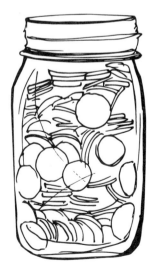

last, entangles our lives, and ultimately won't satisfy. Don't walk away from His love because you're unwilling to trust Him. He has more for you than you can imagine both in heaven and on the earth you now tread upon.

Jesus was exposing the idols of the rich young ruler's heart to show him how incapable the ruler was of saving himself. After the rich young ruler walked away sorrowful, the disciples wanted to know how in the world anyone could be saved (enter God's kingdom)—especially people who have their trust in wealth! Jesus then responded with those life-saving, fear-releasing, hope-giving words: what is completely impossible for us is possible with God.

When we realize we're not good enough, regardless of what we are trusting in, this is precisely where Jesus meets us—at the point of our reckoning how incapable we are to save ourselves.

Whether you're clinging to your wealth, heritage, or your ability to be a good person to get you into heaven, I want to make clear the good news of the gospel that Jesus was pointing to. He was demonstrating the sheer impossibility of our ability to keep all of God's commandments perfectly. He was saying we can't rely on our achievements or self-effort. He made the case that no matter how righteous we think we are, we still lack one thing—total trust in Him. This is why Jesus died on the cross to pay for our sin and bear the penalty that should have been ours. This is why He specifically stated that salvation is impossible for us but possible with God. And what the rich young ruler didn't understand is that the Jesus he'd called "Good Teacher" was God Himself and would be that salvation.

PERSONAL RESPONSE: If today you recognize for the first time that your goodness is not enough, would you pray this prayer and begin your relationship with Jesus? You'll discover that what's impossible for you is possible with Him.

Dear heavenly Father, thank You for Your goodness in sending Jesus Christ. Thank You that He kept the law perfectly from His heart. I confess that I cannot be the righteousness that You require and now believe that righteousness only comes from Jesus. Through His death and resurrection, I find my salvation in Him.

Looking at them, Jesus said, "With man it is impossible, but not with God, because all things are possible with God."
Mark 10:27

DAY FIVE
THE GOD
WHO PROVIDES

GENESIS 22:12b: Now I know that you fear God, because you have not withheld from me your son, your only son (NIV).

Today we'll look at one of the most uncomfortable scenes in the Bible—God calling Abraham to sacrifice his son Isaac. Though the story is difficult, it is also rewarding. I, along with countless others, have wrestled with this account. One question we ask: how can a good God ask such a thing? While this and other questions may not be fully answered, here are a few helpful truths to keep in mind before we read today's passage.

In ancient Hebrew culture, the firstborn had special significance. Ancient cultures were not as individualistic as cultures are today—everything was about the family. The law of primogeniture was in place, meaning that nearly the entire inheritance went to the firstborn son, making him a benefactor for everyone else.[1] "Ancient cultures [looked] to the firstborn as the ultimate hope of the family."[2]

God, however, required that every firstborn be offered to Him (Ex. 13:2). The life of the firstborn was always redeemed by an offering (Num. 3:40-51; 18:14-16). Also notice that God did not ask Abraham to murder his son but to offer him as a sacrifice. While still strange to our modern-day ears, I mention this context because part of what makes this story difficult to grasp is that we live in a vastly different culture.[3] That said, nothing mitigates how painful and unthinkable this task was for Abraham. Before reading today's passage, ask the Lord to help you see this story in a fresh, redeeming light. If you're familiar with it, don't rush—take it slow.

READ GENESIS 22:1-18.

PERSONAL TAKE: Look back at verse 5. Why do you think Abraham said that Isaac would return with him given what God had asked Abraham to do?

To not scare Isaac/him run away

or

He truly believed God would keep him safe.

How did the angel know Abraham feared God (v. 12)?

He was willing to give up his only Son— his inheritance // 1st born

Why did the angel say God would bless Abraham (vv. 16-17)?

Because he trusted in God's provision—he OBEYED.

The word *withheld* jumped out at me during my reading of this passage. Consider the ordeal of planning the sacrifice, the three-day journey, the wood and fire, the fear and confusion Isaac experienced, and the unspeakable grief and wonder Abraham must have gone through. All of it came down to this one choice: to withhold or not withhold.

> *How did Abraham's choice not to withhold his treasure from the Lord affect all of history?*

PERSONAL REFLECTION: Is there something the Lord is asking you to no longer withhold from Him? What's holding you back?

Part of what makes this whole study so precious to me is its deeply personal subject matter. I remember reading about Abraham and Isaac in the middle of my painful journey of laying down precious relationships and a career I loved. My emotional well-being and daily fulfillment hinged upon these things. I honestly wasn't sure if my life would have meaning without them. The scary part was that God asked me to lay them down before He showed me what He would provide in their place. Some things He graciously gave back; others He did not. But in both cases, it was all for my good and His glory. All these years later, I can say with certainty: there's not a sliver I would take back if it meant forsaking His presence.

Understanding the difference between letting something go and making it an offering has been instrumental in my process of "laying down" my idols. We should completely let go of things such as blatant sins and relationships outside the bounds of God's blessings. In fact, we need to run for our lives from them (1 Cor. 6:18; 2 Tim. 2:22). However, there are other things the Lord simply wants us to place on the altar as an offering to Him, as Abraham did with Isaac. This would include any good thing in our lives that has become a consuming or ultimate thing: food, relationships, entertainment, money, or our homes. Certain gods we need to lay down, others need to be offered up.

PERSONAL REFLECTION: What do you need to completely let go of, and what needs to be offered up? For instance, a sinful relationship or habit needs to go, plain and simple. But you may need to put a person, job, or good pleasure that has too powerful a place in your life on the altar as an offering to the Lord.

A. W. Tozer's *The Pursuit of God* is a Christian classic containing a chapter entitled "The Blessedness of Possessing Nothing." I love this excerpt from the chapter as it relates to our reading today about Abraham and Isaac.

> Abraham was old when Isaac was born, old enough to have been his grandfather, and the child became at once the delight and idol of his heart. From the moment he first stooped to take the tiny form awkwardly in his arms, he was an eager love slave of his son. God went out of His way to comment on the strength of this affection. And it is not hard to understand. The baby represented everything sacred to his father's heart: the promises of God, the covenants, the hopes of the years and the long messianic dream. As he watched him grow from babyhood to young manhood, the heart of the old man was knit closer and closer with the life of his son, till at last the relationship bordered upon the perilous. It was then that God stepped in to save both father and son from the consequences of an uncleansed love.[4]
>
> *Had you ever considered Isaac as an "idol" of Abraham's, as Tozer refers to him? Do you agree or disagree? Why?*

TURN TO HEBREWS 11:17-19.

How did Abraham believe God was going to handle his dilemma? How does this provide insight to your answer to the Personal Take on page 133?

Tozer says: "We are often hindered from giving up our treasures to the Lord out of fear for their safety … But we need have no such fears. Our Lord came not to destroy but to save. Everything is safe which we commit to Him, and nothing is really safe which is not so committed." [5]

How often our fears, selfishness, and lack of trust in Jesus and His promises keep us from offering our dearest treasures to Him. We're also contending with Satan and the strands of our culture that tell us we'll miss out and be miserable if we surrender our false gods. If you're like me, you're certain that the minute you pray that prayer of offering, your house will burn down and you'll be sent overseas to minister out of a hut. Or God will make you fall in love with your weirdest, most unattractive, single neighbor. I'm here to hold up these next verses as a much more reliable standard as to what can happen when we give our all to the Lord.

> **REREAD GENESIS 22:13-18.**
>
> *What did Abraham name the place of the sacrifice? Why do you think he called it that?*

If you're afraid to relinquish control of something to the Lord, I hope the fact that God is referred to here as Jehovah-Jireh—"The LORD Will Provide"— brings you assurance. Being a provider is part of His nature. Also, I hope you were encouraged by the incomparable blessings God poured out on Abraham as a result of his obedience.

There is nothing we can lay down that God cannot provide something better in its place.

There is nothing we can lay down that God cannot provide something better in its place. There is nothing we can lay down that God cannot resurrect. Remember Jesus' words from Mark 10:29-30 that we looked at yesterday. He will give back abundantly anything we give up for the sake of the gospel— both in heaven and in this lifetime.

> *Whether you're ready to lay down one thing or a few things, consider using this prayer I've prayed a few monumental times in my life. Again, A. W. Tozer (I just haven't found anyone who says it better.):*

Father, I want to know Thee, but my cowardly heart fears to give up its toys. I cannot part with them without inward bleeding, and I do not try to hide from Thee the terror of the parting. I come trembling, but I do come. Please root from my heart all those things which I have cherished so long and which have become a very part of my living self, so that Thou mayest enter and dwell there without a rival. Then shalt Thou make the place of Thy feet glorious. Then shall my heart have no need of the sun to shine in it, for Thyself wilt be the light of it, and there shall be no night there. In Jesus' name. Amen. [6]

READ ROMANS 8:31-32.

As Abraham did not withhold his only son, Isaac, so God our Father did not spare His only Son, Jesus. Though the angels held back Abraham's arm as he was about to strike his son, there were no angels breaking through the sky to hold back the cross. While a ram in the thicket would be provided for Abraham, no sacrifice apart from the Lamb of God who takes away the sin of the world would do for our salvation. Because of God's great love for us, He did not withhold His Son. In the precious words of Tim Keller, "If Abraham had been at the foot of Calvary the moment that Jesus died, you know what he would have done? He would have taken the words of God to him in verse twelve and turned them around. And he would have looked up at the Father and he would have said, 'Now I know, now I know, now I know that You love me. Because You did not withhold Your Son, Your only Son whom You love from me.'"[7]

Yesterday we looked at how the rich young ruler withheld his wealth from Jesus and missed the incomparable blessing of knowing and following Him. If you still haven't come to that place of entrusting your whole life to Jesus—withholding nothing from Him—ask the Lord to do the impossible in you. Withhold nothing from Him because He withheld nothing from you—not even His only Son, Jesus Christ.

SESSION SIX VIEWER GUIDE

They can NEVER TOUCH the promises of GOD!!!

SAYING GOODBYE TO SAY HELLO

people
relationships
dreams
careers
money
} Things that are good that can become bad.

• Our idea of idols are always better than the reality of them.

Heb. 11:6 — god rewards those who step out in faith → to leave IDOLS
Gen 17:17-18,19 — "If only Ishmael were under your blessing"
Faith is believing
1. What God is calling us to is infinitely better than what were being asked to leave behind

≡ What am I nurturing? Being mindful of? ≡
≡ Is it Keeping me in bondage to idols? ≡
✱ Don't leave yourself room to turn back...
   Rom. 16:19

2. Faith is barricading the road that leads back to captivity by not nurturing thoughts of the path

GROUP DISCUSSION

What one thing from this video teaching really resonated with you? Why?

Why do we struggle to obey God when we can't see the next step?

How do you exercise faith in the small things of your life, the everyday, practical things? Is it more difficult to exercise faith in the crises or the mundane? Explain.

How does dwelling on and cultivating thoughts from the past open up the door for you to return there (Heb. 11:15)?

What things in your past do you find most difficult to leave behind? What do you continue to dwell on, perhaps unrighteously?

Do you truly believe that identifying with Christ is the joy and reward of your life? If so, what is the evidence? If not, why not?

What is God asking you to leave behind today? What's keeping you from doing so?

3. Faith is not allowing fear determine / direct the future God has for me.

≡ Don't seek the FLEETING pleasures of SIN! ≡
Fear keeps us in BONDAGE to our IDOLS!

Video sessions available for purchase or rent at LIFEWAY.COM/NOOTHERGODS

#NOOTHERGODS

Homemade Pizza (makes 2-3 small pizzas)

INGREDIENTS:

Crust:

1½ cups warm water (see note)

1 package dry yeast

7 tablespoons olive oil, divided

1½ teaspoons salt

1 teaspoon granulated sugar

4 cups all-purpose flour, divided

Cooking spray

Toppings:

1 tablespoon olive oil

2 garlic cloves, minced

1 (14-ounce) jar pizza sauce

2 cups shredded mozzarella cheese

Pepperoni or sausage

Favorite veggies

MAKE THE CRUST

In a large bowl, dissolve yeast in warm water. Add 3 tablespoons of olive oil, salt, and sugar. Stir. Add 2 cups of the flour. Beat with a mixer, or mix with wooden spoon. Then, add remaining 2 cups flour, one at a time, mixing as you go. Knead until smooth, about 5 minutes. Place dough in an olive-oil-greased bowl, brush the top of the dough with olive oil, and cover with a damp cloth. Place in a warm oven (80-90 degrees) for about an hour. (I heat the oven just a little, then turn it off, and place bowl in oven. Be careful—if it's too hot the dough will begin to bake.) After the dough rises, punch it down. (Push your fist gently and firmly into the middle of the dough. Then, wrap the edges of the dough into its center, creating a ball.) Sprinkle your countertop with flour, and lightly roll out the dough. Place dough onto lightly greased pizza pan. Brush dough with the remaining olive oil, if desired. Let rise again for an hour. (You can omit this step if you wish.) Once dough has risen to your satisfaction, cover with your favorite pizza toppings.

Note: The water that is added to the yeast should be quite warm, almost hot, but not so hot that it burns you. If it's not hot enough, the dough won't rise. If it is too hot, it will kill the yeast!

ASSEMBLE THE PIZZA

Preheat oven to 425 degrees.

Spread olive oil over dough and sprinkle with garlic. Add your favorite pizza sauce. (I like to use a 32-ounce can of whole San Marzano tomatoes, slightly puree them, and add salt.) Layer shredded mozzarella over tomato sauce, and add your favorite toppings (pepperoni, sausage, and/or your favorite veggies).

Place pizza in preheated oven, and bake for approximately 10 minutes or until the cheese is melted and the crust is golden brown. This baking time will vary considerably depending on the oven.

Homemade pizza is not only the best tasting meal that all ages can agree on, but it's also a really fun social activity. When I make pizza with my family and friends we roll, toss, chop, and sprinkle while talking about our weeks. It's not just dinner, it's an activity. If you're making this for your Bible study, invite everyone over and cook it together. (Have your dough ready before your Bible study friends arrive.)

NO OTHER GOD CAN DO THIS

I recently witnessed my first total solar eclipse. It swept over Nashville in full regalia, drawing locals and travelers out into fields and up onto rooftops to witness what everyone was calling a once-in-a-lifetime event. The next total eclipse where I live will occur on August 15, 2566—sadly, I have plans to be dead. My friend, Mary Katharine, called me the morning of the big event to give me a solar eclipse pep talk. Knowing I was busy and scattered she rightly implored me: "Pay attention to what's happening today. The Lord went to a lot of trouble to make this happen for us." She was right. The heavens declare His glory, and I best lay my trifling concerns aside and look up.

My sister-in-law's parents, Jim and Lin, flew in for the occasion. Jim is a space enthusiast, which worked out great for me because this meant he pretty much took care of all the preparations. He staked out our spot in the field four hours beforehand, secured our NASA glasses, spread out refreshments on a picnic table, and most importantly, procured the Moon Pies®. When a once-in-five-hundred-years event comes to town, I recommend partying with the experts.

Up until this day, I'd witnessed one or two partial eclipses. But nothing could prepare me for the phenomenon that is the moon fully blocking the sun. The difference between a shaving of sunlight and none at all is starker than you might imagine. In Nashville, totality was reached at 1:27 p.m., lasting nearly two minutes. In the precious hour leading up to this moment we witnessed the moon steadily slide across the sun until a burning red crescent was all that was left, then a mere sliver, then total blackout. For one minute and fifty-five seconds the moon hung her cloak in front of the sun, covering its fiery ball with aplomb. The temperature dropped, the heavens fell dim, and the glow of a sunset appeared in every direction you could cast your gaze. The sky was silvery dark, but unlike our familiar versions of dusk or twilight—a total eclipse has its own brand of darkness.

We threw off our glasses and for a short duration beheld the spectacle unfiltered. Bare-eyed I saw the Bailey's Beads Effect, the flecks of light that pass through the moon's mountainous terrain. I saw the corona waltzing around the edges of the moon's disc. My nephew, Will, thrust his fist in the air, letting out a boyish howl at the sight. Spectators cheered in unison, applauding the display we had no part in creating. Our only job that day was to behold.

I don't know what it is about our daily concerns, the harried running to and fro, even the formidable persistent trials that keep us from worshipping the Creator of the universe. Too often, I take for granted that the Lord fashioned the heavens and the earth, the sea and the dry land, the mountain peaks and rainforests, the moon, sun, stars, and the solar eclipse.

This is the same Lord to whom David exclaimed, "What is man that you are mindful of him?" (Ps. 8:4, ESV). When I take the time to meditate on God's greatness in the psalms, when I worship Him with adoration, when I fall before Him in prayer, my cares come into proper perspective. My priorities fall into order. My idols prove downright silly in comparison.

The moon continued to plod west to east, pausing not nearly long enough for us to begin to comprehend what we were seeing. Just like that, the sun's rays slipped out from behind the other side of the moon. By 3:00 p.m. the eclipse was over. But the magnitude of what we'd all witnessed, the display of God's splendor, would remain with me forever. Our false gods may promise the world, but our God created it, sustains it, and rules over it. And no other god can do that.

and false gods offer FLEETING pleasures.

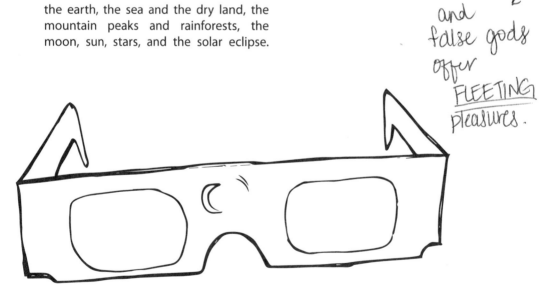

DAY ONE
HE SATISFIES YOUR LONGINGS

10-07-2019

ISAIAH 55:1: Come, all you who are thirsty, come to the waters; and you who have no money, come, buy and eat! Come, buy wine and milk without money and without cost (NIV).

Years ago, a friend of mine who owns a guitar shop took me on a road trip to pick up twenty-eight high-end guitars from a private collector and player who was liquidating his stash. When we arrived at the man's house, he took us into his basement where we began flipping latches to see what each guitar case held. The owner would point to a case, scratch his forehead and say, "I'm pretty sure I paid over $6,000 for this one, but I've never seen it." Thinking I misunderstood him the first time, I replied, "You mean you've never played it?"

"No, I've never seen it," he said. "I've had it two years and I've never even opened the case." The guy was strange, no doubt about it, but the spiritual analogy stayed with me.

To have over $100,000 worth of guitar inventory that he'd never even seen, forget about played, was reminiscent of the way I'd been living. Jesus Christ and His blessings were freely accessible to me, but I'd been looking elsewhere. During this season, I was entangled with idols I was sure would fulfill me but weren't. Meanwhile I was having a hard time opening the extraordinary treasure of God's Word, much less enjoying its songs.

Today we'll see the Israelites in a similar place. But instead of sitting on a pile of expensive guitars they'd never bothered to look at, they were missing out on a feast the Lord had prepared for them.

READ ISAIAH 55:1-7.

PERSONAL REFLECTION: This chapter reads like poetry. What line stands out to you the most and why?

"why do you spend money for that which is not bread, and labor for that which doesn't satisfy?"

What kinds of people does the Lord call to Himself?

"EVERYONE" (v. 1)

The ultimate question. Why do we run to idols/ and not GOD?

The Israelites were spending their silver and wages on what did not

~~SATISFY~~.

Why do we spend our money on stuff that doesn't satisfy us? Why do we flit away our time on things that don't matter? Why are our resources and mental energies and daydreaming consumed by what can never fulfill us? These questions are perplexing at first glance. Who consciously buys things they don't want or spends their time on what they don't desire? No one. That would be insanity. But notice that these verses aren't about what we want, rather they focus on what will satisfy us. Herein lies a great misunderstanding: We assume the things we want are synonymous with what will satisfy our longings. But that is not always the case.

We assume the things we want are synonymous with what will satisfy our longings. But that is not always the case.

WOW.
Yes - I assumed the same.
This thinking makes us believe we know what's best...

PERSONAL REFLECTION: Last week you reflected on getting something you really wanted that didn't end up satisfying you. It could be a possession or a relationship. In light of today's reading, why do you think the people and things we want often don't satisfy? Take time to reflect on this.

Possibly bc its not what were *really* needing. We search for the TANGIBLE / FEELINGS to grasp...

Isaiah 55 begins with the word come. *What two other imperatives (commands) are used in verses 2 and 3?*

"LISTEN"
"COME"

[highlighted] The only way to discover what will truly satisfy us is by coming to the Lord and listening to Him, paying close attention to what He has to teach us through His Word. [end highlight] He is the One who tells us the truth about where real nourishment comes from. He leads us to the true feast.

In Isaiah 55:1-3, God says "Come," "Listen," and "Pay attention." Next to each imperative, write the promises attached to them.

COME	there is no price
LISTEN	eat what is good; delight yourself
PAY ATTENTION	so that your soul may live

↳ We look for things for our

[margin] ¹Come, everyone who is thirsty, come to the water; and you without silver, come, buy, and eat! Come, buy wine and milk without silver and without cost! ² Why do you spend silver on what is not food, and your wages on what does not satisfy? Listen carefully to me, and eat what is good, and you will enjoy the choicest of foods. ³ Pay attention and come to me; listen, so that you will live.
Isaiah 55:1-3

PERSONAL TAKE: Why do you think God uses the imagery of choice food, wine, and milk that's free of cost to illustrate the life He offers us?

physical needs not our spiritual needs

I believe God had material blessings He desired to give to Israel, but more than anything He was offering them soul food. (Or maybe I should say food for the soul, in case you just went straight to fried chicken, purple-hull peas, turnip greens, and fried okra.) Our souls don't need to starve anymore because God fulfilled the covenant He'd made with David and his throne (2 Sam. 7:12-16) described in Isaiah 55:3-5, with the coming of Jesus, the promised Messiah. And isn't spiritual starvation often what propels us to false gods? We yearn for attention but don't get it the way we want, so we soothe our aches by losing ourselves in fantasy worlds online. We feel inferior so we turn to the gods of materialism to keep up. We long for intimacy, so we attempt to satiate our desires through sexual activity outside the covenant of marriage, or we lose ourselves in a false online world of people who don't truly know us. We're lonely so we overeat to fill the void. We feel worthless, so we disproportionately throw ourselves into our work to feel valuable. Still, we are not satiated.

Turn to Jeremiah 2:13. What two sins had the Israelites committed?

> 1. Forsook God
> 2. Hewed out cisterns for themselves

PERSONAL REFLECTION: Specifically describe how your primary false god has failed to hold water for you? Why have you not looked to God, the spring of living water?

> Getting recognition from ppl / attention from men *may* satisfy my ego or allow me to feel good for a few hours, BUT never truly ends my craving — not satisfying.

Isaiah 55 begins with an urgent call to those in the endless cycle of drawing water and pouring it into broken cisterns, to those who are thirsty and without resources. Our affluence heightens one of the greatest deterrents to our faith—rarely realizing just how thirsty and poor we are. We have so much to entertain and distract us that we can literally go years without recognizing that our souls are starving for true nourishment and thirsting for the pure living water the Lord offers.

PERSONAL REFLECTION: Where is your soul thirsty or poor right now? Be specific.

> Honestly, right now, I'm having a hard time identifying where I'm soul thirsty ... I feel very connected to the Lord.

Look up the following passages and explain how each one shows Jesus to be the fulfillment of the prophetic word from Isaiah 55.

John 4:13-14

Jesus gives life-giving water.

John 6:32-35

The Father's bread gives life

Romans 6:23

Gods FREE gift is eternal life.
(Es 55:1)

Revelation 22:16-17

If you are thirsty "come" - w/o
Price. FREE GIFT.

It pains me to think of the time and energy I've spent over the years trying to grasp what could never satisfy me. I've spun my wheels, manipulated my circumstances, balanced on wires, tried to keep plates in the air, flitted away time on my phone, and spent my resources all for what I thought would fulfill me but didn't. And couldn't. We need not live another day this way.

READ ISAIAH 55:6-7 AGAIN.

PERSONAL RESPONSE: The Lord gives a few more imperatives in these verses. I've listed them below. Next to each one, detail how you will respond accordingly. Some might apply more than others.

Seek the Lord:

continue in daily Bible reading
cont. in Bible studies

Call to Him:

pray more often

Abandon your sinful ways and thoughts:

reflect on my actions, ask forgiveness,
and turn.

Return to the Lord:

keep turning toward God

Recognize this passage as a compassionate call to repentance, allowing us to enjoy the abundance and richest of fare that comes with Christ as the center of our lives.

If your soul is thirsty, come to Jesus. If you're craving real spiritual food, listen to His words in the pages of Scripture. If you're looking for life that's truly life, pay attention to what He has to say and then keep in step with His loving instruction.

If your soul is thirsty, come to Jesus.

If you don't have the world's silver or if you've got all this world has to offer, but you're spending it on what can't possibly nourish your hungry heart, come to the feast where Jesus offers a meal only His blood could purchase. Return to the Lord. He longs to have compassion on you. He longs to freely forgive.

PERSONAL RESPONSE: If you need to repent of a false god, end today's study with a prayer of repentance. If your conscience is pure before the Lord, end with a prayer of thanksgiving and worship.

DAY TWO
HE RESCUES YOU

PSALM 18:16: He reached down from on high and took hold of me; He pulled me out of deep water.

Recently, I caught a glimpse of a television show while waiting for an appointment. Unfortunately, the people on this show were very loudly discussing every conceivable dysfunction in front of a live audience—and incidentally, all the people stuck in waiting rooms across the country. Since there was only one other woman in the room, I thought about asking if someone could turn the volume down or change the channel. I'd had a long few weeks and wondered if we could find something closer to *The Sound of Music*. That's when the other woman exclaimed from her chair, "Can you turn this up? I want to hear how this ends!" A little part of my heart shriveled.

On the program, a husband and wife were hashing out their marital problems, even dragging their daughter's pain onto national television. The wife wanted to be rescued from her raging husband. He wanted out of being married to a liar. The child was held hostage in the middle. Everyone on the show was talking over each other, the audience was hooting and hollering, and the lady next to me was glued to the screen. It was the most unnerving, anxiety-ridden hour I've had with strangers in a while. All I could see were three people who desperately needed rescuing. And while the host had some helpful things to say, he was nowhere close to being able to save them.

Throughout Israel's history we often see the people of God turning from their true Rescuer to the false gods of other nations. We discovered in our first week of study that Israel stands as an example from which we can learn. If I have one prayer for you today, it's that you'll discover how able our Savior is to rescue. No other person or thing can compare.

In the words of C. H. Spurgeon,

> If thou hast anything that perplexes thee, the simplest plan for thee will be, not to try to solve the difficulty, but to seek direction from heaven concerning it. If thou hast, at this moment, some doubt that is troubling thee, thy wisest plan will be, not to combat the doubt, but to come to Christ just as thou art, and to refer the doubt to him. Remember how men act when they are

concerned in a lawsuit; if they are wise, they do not undertake the case themselves. They know our familiar proverb, "He who is his own lawyer has a fool for his client;" so they take their case to someone who is able to deal with it, and leave it with him.[1]

PERSONAL RESPONSE: Before going any further, present yourself to God, leaving all your struggles, issues, and doubts with Him. He is able.

READ JEREMIAH 2:1-13.

In a few sentences, summarize Israel's offense.

They went away from the Lord. They defiled the land. They hewed out cisterns for themselves — forsaking God.

According to verses 6-7, list what the Lord had delivered Israel from and what He'd delivered them to.

From Egypt/wilderness/darkness INTO fruitful/ Plentiful land

Look at verse 11. What unique exchange had Israel made? Have you ever witnessed anything like this in culture or in your personal life? If so, describe.

Glory for things that do not profit. Gods for no gods.

PERSONAL REFLECTION: In verse 2, what did the Lord remember about Israel? Can you think of a time when you followed closely to the Lord through a wilderness experience?

→ Yes. Alone throughout college. I found my ultimate friend & Comforter in Jesus.

Their devotion, their love, how they followed.

I often wonder what causes people to fall out of deep intimacy with the Lord. How desperately I want to finish more in love with Him than when I first believed. I imagine it's the same for you too. And yet we've probably all known people who began their relationship with Christ excited and sold out but are no longer following Him. Maybe you've experienced being distant from Him in your own life. In this passage, the Lord gives us insight into why this takes place.

What question did the Lord ask in verse 5? And what questions had the Israelites stopped asking (vv. 6-8)?

fathers

v5 "what wrong did you find in me?"

V.6-8 "where is the Lord?"

I love the Word of God for its penetrating questions. After the Lord had delivered Israel out of slavery in Egypt, after leading them through the wilderness, after bringing them into the promised land and miraculously defeating their enemies, they turned to false gods and the prophets of Baal. Then the Lord asked, "What fault did your fathers find in me?" (v. 5).

PERSONAL RESPONSE: Are you holding the Lord responsible for something that's happened in your life? A disappointment? Something that's propelled you toward another god? Explain.

I have - and probably still do.

Simultaneously, have you forgotten the good things He's done for you, including the past deliverance He's brought you? Explain.

At times yes. But I'm reminded he's a good father. Never fails!

We're continually tempted to look to the gods of our culture for rescue, but the psalms in particular remind us that Almighty God is the only One with the power to save. Let the following passages breathe confidence and hope into your soul as you're reminded of the God who delights in rescuing His people.

READ PSALM 18:16-19 AND 142:5-7.

What does God rescue His people out of and into?

Out of deep waters/hands of the enemy. Brought me into a broad place.

READ PSALM 68:4-6.

What kinds of people in particular does God care for and rescue?

Fatherless
Widows   *Prisoners*

I waited patiently for the LORD, and he turned to me and heard my cry for help.
Psalm 40:1

READ PSALM 40:1-5.

How does waiting for God's rescue play a part in this psalm? If you've been waiting for a long time, in what ways does this psalm encourage you?

Psalmist says he waited PATIENTLY and God heard his cry.

Often in the waiting our strength fails, our hope fades, and we turn to false gods we believe will instantaneously save us. Or at least numb the pain. If I have any encouragement for you, it's don't give up on the faithfulness of the Lord. Patient waiting develops character, perspective, and slow-growing blessings that often outshine the very thing we're waiting for.

Psalm 46:10-11 in the CSB says, "Stop your fighting, and know that I am God, exalted among the nations, exalted on the earth. The LORD of Armies is with us; the God of Jacob is our stronghold."

What can we stop doing because of God's strength to deliver?

Stop worrying
Trying to take things into our own hands.

The NASB translates the first phrase "cease striving." Is there any area of your life in which you need to cease striving, give up the fight, and put your trust in the Lord? Explain.

READ PSALM 146:1-10.

How do the most powerful of humans, those in whom we tend to put our trust, compare to the Lord Almighty?

You've read a lot of Scripture today. I pray God's words have not only washed over you but also sunk deeply into your souls. I've needed the reminder of who God is, what He's done, and what He promises to do. In your season of trial don't forsake Him for all the lesser things that have no power to rescue. Instead, lift up your head to the King of glory. "Who is he, this King of glory? The LORD of Armies, he is the King of glory" (Ps. 24:10).

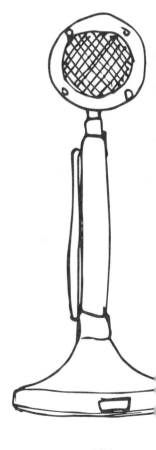

HE TAKES AWAY YOUR SIN AND SHAME

ISAIAH 54:4a: Do not be afraid, for you will not be put to shame; don't be humiliated, for you will not be disgraced.

The jungle pastors and their wives, the courageous men and women who serve in the Amazon, streamed up the side of the hill for Justice & Mercy International's annual Jungle Pastor's Conference in Brazil. Many of them I already knew. But every year we meet fresh faces whose smiles give way to incomprehensible stories. Daniel's story would prove no different.

"Pastora Sarah," he whispered. "May I speak with you?" Sarah is our national director.

"Of course, Pastor. Over here." He shuffled across the lawn, a body of shy bones following her to an out-of-the-way corner.

"Sarah, I need you to know something about me before this conference begins." He could only lock eyes with her for a fraction of a glance.

"Pastor, go on," she affirmed with her hand on his shoulder.

"I can't read" he murmured. "My wife told me we had to come, but I don't know what I'm doing here."

Daniel wore the shame of his illiteracy as though it were a permanent uniform. The embarrassment he bore was crippling. Sarah assured him he'd come to the right place. The Jungle Pastor's Conference is full of broken believers, each having been delivered from all manner of shame, guilt, and sin, while still in the process of being delivered. It's my favorite place on earth.

The thing about shame is that sometimes it's tied to our sin, but other times it's simply a result of circumstances, as in Daniel's case. Either way, shame is one of those conditions that reaches into our souls and robs us of who God has made us to be, holding us back from what He's created us to do. The enemy will try to keep us stuck in our shame and guilt by convincing us it's all too much for God, that we're past His ability to redeem. At that point, we're only a step away from turning back to the false gods who mask our shame and affirm our sin.

My prayer today is that you'll know beyond any doubt that we serve a God who delights to take away our shame. No other god can do that.

READ ISAIAH 54:1-5 THREE TIMES THROUGH, MEDITATING ON THE DIFFERENT IMAGERY. *Keep in mind that the barren or childless one refers to Zion or Jerusalem.*

barren
married/
husband
tents/cords

READ GENESIS 30:22-23 AND NEHEMIAH 2:17.

Describe what caused disgrace in each situation.

① *Being barren*
② *Ruins of Jerusalem/burned*

Zion is referred to here in feminine form because she is pictured as God's bride. (Later in the New Testament we see God's church as the bride of Christ.) She is also described as barren, most likely because of her recent captivity in Babylon and the way she strayed from the Lord. She was unable to bear the spiritual fruit the Lord had intended for her because she turned her back on God. But things were about to change.

In what ways did God want her to prepare? List everything mentioned in verse 2. ① *Enlarge your tent*
② *Let curtains be stretched out*
③ *Don't hold back*   ④ *Lengthen cords/strengthen stakes*

In ancient Near Eastern culture, if a husband and wife wanted to increase the number of their children, they'd enlarge their tent to make room for those children.[2] In the same way, the Lord was declaring a huge shift for Israel. He was promising an enormous increase of His people returning home, as well as new people coming to know the one true God. The Lord didn't want Israel to prepare sparsely. In modern-day terms it'd be: draw up the plans, get the addition going, open up the kitchen, fill the pantry, hang the porch lights. The party is about to get started.

PERSONAL TAKE: According to verse 4, what might have held Zion back from taking this step of faith, from believing this was possible?

They were afraid and confused.

I love this quote by Gary Smith, "Now, even before the promise is fulfilled, the prophet encourages the woman to respond in faith and in anticipation of God's great love."[3] Can I get an amen?

PERSONAL REFLECTION: What keeps you from "spreading out your tent" when it comes to living for God's kingdom? In other words, what holds you back from preparing for the spiritual increase the Lord wants to bring about in your life? *Well, am I aware of it when God is trying to "spread my tent"??*

It's hard to know what specific instance the author had in mind when referring to Israel's disgrace. Whether her captivity in Egypt, exile to Babylon, worship of Baal, or her seasons of turning her back on the Lord, God was clear about how He wanted her to treat those memories. She was to forget them and stop dwelling on those failures.

PERSONAL REFLECTION: Look back at verses 4-5. What keeps you from forgetting painful memories and moving on from past failures?

Remembering them can keep you angry & feel in control.
You may never want it to happen again, so you hold on to it to avoid a re-do

God's gracious proclamation over Zion about her physical and spiritual multiplication was not because her sins didn't matter, or enough time had passed and God was finally over it, or He woke up one day with amnesia. The reason Israel could move on from her past and embrace the abundance of her future is found in Isaiah 53.

READ ISAIAH 53:1-12.

Who does this passage appear to be speaking about?

JESUS!

PERSONAL REFLECTION: Look at verses 5, 6, and 11 from Isaiah 53. How does Jesus make possible God's promise to bless Zion despite her sin? How is this true for you as well?

We NO longer need to carry it!

God has put all our sin onto Jesus — who bore it on the cross!

Isn't it true that our shame is what so often keeps us from spreading our tent, driving those pegs deep into the ground, and making room for ministry while anticipating God's blessing? We're afraid we'll be known for who we really are, certain we'll be disqualified. We decide we can't let go of the shame of our youth, so we turn to false gods that affirm our sinful choices.

READ HEBREWS 12:1-2.

What did Jesus despise about the cross, and what was one reason He endured it?

despised the shame
endured it for the joy set before him

It's time to stop dwelling on your past shame, time to shed those old garments and make room for God's abundant blessings.

It's time to stop dwelling on your past shame, time to shed those old garments and make room for God's abundant blessings. It's time to stop using your past as an excuse to stay in your comfort zone and keep your tent pegs where they are. The reason any of us are able to move on from our past sin and shame is because of what Jesus did for us on the cross. No other god can do that. The redemption cost was too great for you to stay in bondage to the sins of your youth—sins you're still practicing or ones that still carry painful residue.

PERSONAL RESPONSE: What is one specific way you can move on from your shame and receive Jesus' invitation to follow Him?

Recognize that when I carry shame, I'm essentially saying that Jesus' wasn't strong enough to take it away/ rejecting the gift that he died for me/ sin!

If you're still wondering how it is possible to "forget your shame," return to Isaiah 54 and revisit verse 5. Fill in the following blanks.

When referring to the one true God, Isaiah said, He is your … and gave three specific roles. What were they?

Your **husband**

Your **Redeemer**

Your **Maker**

When we said goodbye to Daniel at the end of our pastor's conference, his countenance beamed. He determined he'd learn how to read this year but not because being able to read would relieve his shame. Rather, his sacred value to Christ and the love we shared for him gave him the strength to not let shame keep him from trying. To be clear, illiteracy is not a sin. Still, all kinds of things—sin or not—bring about shame that keeps us from our calling. Because of Jesus, let's not spend another minute languishing in our shame. Instead, let's embrace our calling, and as Gary Smith put it, let's "respond in faith and in anticipation of God's great love."[4]

DAY FOUR
HE'S THE ONE
YOU CAN TRUST

DANIEL 3:16: Shadrach, Meshach and Abednego
replied to the king, "King Nebuchadnezzar, we do not
need to defend ourselves before you in this matter" (NIV).

In the original study, I wrote, "Making room is why we've been turning from our false gods. It's the ambition of our hard and sometimes painful work. I think my heart would just stop beating if I didn't have the belief that as I clear out the lesser idols I'm making space for the living God. Many people have made room for God in stunning measures, stood back, and watched Him overflow the space. You or I cannot be the exception."

As I reflect on these words over a decade later I could weep at how the living God has filled the space He asked me to create. Indeed it is overflowing. While I'm thankful for the material blessings He's given, it's the friendships, ministry opportunities, peace, deep intimacy with the Savior, my local church, and the quiet gifts He's given that have so overwhelmed me. I'm also moved by the sober understanding that I could have missed God's blessings if I had allowed the <u>loneliness and heartache that often accompany</u> walking <u>away from false gods to deter me</u>—the stuff that tempts us to turn back.

I feel as though our minds magnify what this world offers.

Regardless of what this world offers, please don't turn back and miss what God has for you. I understand that empty space you're clearing out can be scary and lonely. <u>But He will fill it in His perfect way and time.</u> It's what He does.

PERSONAL REFLECTION: Since we began our study together, in what area(s) of your life have you removed idols to begin creating room for God? Has the process left any empty spaces of loneliness?

I've noticed I've moved away from the idol of comparison.

Other idols like social media are extremely hard to stay away from—you want to be connect and be relevant.

Today we'll look at three men who stood strong in the face of the overwhelming temptation to worship the gods of their culture. Their stand left them isolated and perhaps, lonely.

Read all of Daniel 3, and look for ways that Shadrach, Meshach, and Abednego made room for God by not bowing down to the false gods of their day.

What was the consequence for not bowing to the statue?
(Circle your answers from the options below.)

Imprisonment   Incineration   Loss of position   Exile

How many others besides Shadrach, Meshach, and Abednego refused to bow down?

What do verses 13 and 19 say about Nebuchadnezzar's temperament?

PERSONAL REFLECTION: Has another person's anger or threats ever made you afraid to stand on your convictions? If so, describe.

Shadrach, Meshach, and Abednego were ultimately alone in their refusal to bow down. Their decision separated them from the rest of the officials. This is a good reminder as one who likes people to be pleased with me. I hate the idea of being divided from those around me, especially people I love. As a result, I have a hard time separating myself based on the convictions the Lord has put in my heart. If I were one of these three men, I wouldn't have wanted to bow down, but I would have wanted to smooth the whole thing over. I would have made sure Neb's feelings weren't hurt and that all the other officials understood where I was coming from. Which brings me to my next note.

Read verses 15-18, and describe Shadrach, Meshach, and Abednego's response to the king. How did they defend themselves?

Verse 16 in the King James Version reads: "Shadrach, Meshach, and Abednego, answered and said to the king, O Nebuchadnezzar, we are not *careful* to answer thee in this matter" (emphasis mine). The Hebrew word for *careful* means *hasty, to have need of, ready.* It implies a sense of urgency and eagerness. In essence, they were saying, "We are not urgent, eager, or pressed to answer or defend ourselves."

Do you give yourself time before responding in the heat of the moment? Sometimes I fight an overwhelming need to explain my decisions, when

Sometimes the best response is a peaceful, humble non-response.

really the best thing to do is quietly rest in my convictions and trust the Lord. Sometimes the best response is a peaceful, humble non-response. Just the other day I was about to make a phone call at 3:40 in the afternoon about something that needed to be settled. I sensed the Holy Spirit tell me to wait until 4:00. I'm pretty sure I checked my phone at 3:46, 3:52, and 3:59. But I waited, and it was the right call—pun absolutely intended. Sometimes I only need 20 minutes, other times I need several days. But the discipline of waiting staves off what is often a hyper-tendency for us to settle things in our own time and on our terms.

PERSONAL RESPONSE: Are you facing a situation where the Lord is asking you to pray, think, and make sure your heart is right before responding? Explain.

Between the moment that Shadrach, Meshach, and Abednego refused to bow down and the moment they were delivered from the furnace, I wonder if they considered a compromise that would spare their lives? Either way, they chose to obey God and trust Him in the waiting—no compromises.

When we refuse to bow our hearts to the functional gods in our lives we inevitably lose that god and all it offers. This initial sense of emptiness can cause us to urgently fill the space with something else or hastily try to control our circumstances—especially if we don't immediately feel God's presence in that space or experience His deliverance on the spot.

PERSONAL TAKE: According to Daniel 3:16-18, the men's response was noticeably calm and controlled despite facing the possibility of two very different outcomes. They had no idea which way things would go. What must they have believed about God—regardless of how He chose to act— that served as their unshakable foundation?

I would love to see your answer. As I've pondered this question in my own heart, I believe their resolve was a result of years of daily trust in God and subsequent obedience to Him. Their response speaks of a deep belief that had grown over time. They knew God was big enough to deliver them, in whatever way He chose, and rested in His ability to work that out.

I want to highlight an especially meaningful truth God showed me from this passage during a time of bondage I wasn't sure I'd ever be free of. A woman from my church was teaching a weekly Bible study at a local coffee shop. The Saturday morning I wandered in she was in Daniel 3. I'll let you discover for yourself what she pointed out.

Look back at Daniel 3:21-23. When the men were thrown into the fire were they bound or free?

Now look at verses 24-25. What must have been the only thing the flames consumed?

The Lord used this to show me His ability to use our fiery trials to burn up what's holding us captive, while keeping us safe from the flames. He's so good to use our trials not to harm us but to set us free.

I appreciate these words from scholar Stephen R. Miller, "Most likely the fourth man in the fire was the angel of the Lord, God himself in the person of his Son Jesus Christ, a view held by many expositors ... It is certainly true that when believers go through fiery trials Christ is with them. The three Hebrews experienced literally the promise, 'When you walk through the fire, you will not be burned; the flames will not set you ablaze' (Isa. 43:2)."[5]

God is so good to use our trials not to harm us but to set us free.

In closing today, I want to highlight the last statement in verse 29 (your translations may vary a bit). Complete this sentence: "... for there is _____ _____ _____ who is able to deliver like this."

PERSONAL REFLECTION: How does this verse encourage you to make room for the one true God?

Today I praise Him. No other god can deliver in this way. Thank you, Jesus. No other god can fill the empty space in our lives like our God. Rest in Him today. Make no defense. Refrain from hasty explanations. Be still and know that He is God.

DAY FIVE
HE PROMISES BLESSING

HEBREWS 11:8: By faith Abraham, when called to go to a place he would later receive as his inheritance, obeyed and went, even though he did not know where he was going (NIV).

Growing up, my family spent most vacations in places secluded in nature. My dad would take us kids on hikes up mountains. (My mom's idea of hiking was meandering in and out of shops in the little towns nearby, so we liked to "hike" with her too.) While our goal was always to reach the top of the mountain—that unmistakable clearing where you could cast your gaze across miles of unobstructed beauty—the journey proved equally as exciting. There was the occasional snake my dad would catch basking on the trail. Or the doe and her fawn crackling through the woods. There was also my unyielding hope of finding an arrowhead—a treasure I thought I'd secured many times. But alas, all those triangular shaped rocks I'd picked up turned out to be, well, triangular shaped rocks. The talks we had along the ascent, the people we met on their way down the trail, and the solitude in between were all joyful parts of the experience. While the ultimate blessing, if you will, was reaching the top of the mountain, a hundred other gifts lay along the path of getting there.

In much the same way, our ultimate destination on this *No Other Gods* journey is the place of healing and freedom from our idols, but there are treasures to be had on the journey. While sometimes the Lord delivers instantaneously from an addiction or attachment, I'm more accustomed to a gradual process of freedom and healing. There's a biblical reason for this.

READ 2 PETER 1:5-7.

How is endurance (perseverance or steadfastness) essential to the other virtues mentioned?

READ JAMES 1:2-4.

What does the testing of our faith produce in us?

We see from these two passages that the endurance it takes to complete our walk of faith is not only what leads us to the blessing, it is part of the blessing itself. We may wish for God to snap His fingers and deliver us instantaneously, but if that happened, we'd miss the gift of developing patience and steadfastness. These traits only come on the hike up the mountain. No one gets endurance without first having endured.

PERSONAL REFLECTION: In dealing head-on with your false gods, what is making it most difficult for you to endure? In other words, what makes you want to give up?

As we look at the road ahead, I want you to be well equipped for the process. The following verses promise blessings (in due time) when we persevere. Though we may not have all the specifics, we can be assured that God will do abundantly more than we can imagine if we don't give up.

READ PSALM 130:5-6.

Based on the psalmist's hope in verse 5, what benefit do you think a season of waiting produces?

READ GALATIANS 6:9.

Describe the certainty and timing of the blessing God gives to those who don't give up doing good.

READ HEBREWS 6:10-12.

How are God's promises to us inherited? And what does God promise not to forget?

READ JAMES 1:3-4.

What do the trials and testing of your faith produce?

READ JAMES 5:7-11.

What inspires a farmer to be patient for the harvest? Give this some thought.

PERSONAL RESPONSE: Earlier today you described your greatest hindrance to patient endurance. How do these verses specifically encourage you to keep pressing on?

Sometimes when the Lord calls us to lay something down, He immediately replaces it with a tangible blessing. Other times we're left feeling broken and empty for a season. We wonder what God is doing and whether or not He's still engaged in our lives. It's during these times we're especially tempted to run back to the idol that provided us with a false sense of hope and comfort. It's also during these times that we need to rehearse the truth.

In the video teaching for Session Six, I briefly talked about Abraham's faith. Now I want you to look at the blessings that accompanied his faith, patience, and perseverance.

READ GENESIS 12:1-4 AND HEBREWS 11:8.

What specifics did God give Abraham about where he was going?

Although Abraham didn't know where he was going, list the promises God made to Him.

PERSONAL TAKE: What do you think God valued as most important in Abraham's heart? (Mark your answer.)

- ❏ *Abraham knowing where he was going*
- ❏ *Abraham being obedient to leave*
- ❏ *Abraham receiving the blessings*
- ❏ *Abraham becoming a great nation*

PERSONAL REFLECTION: Can you think of a time when God asked you to turn away from something but wasn't as specific about where/what He was leading you to? If so, briefly write about it.

I believe Abraham's obedience was more important than any other detail—even more important than knowing where he was headed. It's along the journey where our faith and endurance are refined. No doubt many of us have gone through times when we did what the Lord asked us to do and then felt dropped at the farthest bus stop in the middle of nowhere. (My journals detail a few of those moments.) Sometimes I interpreted those experiences as God's punishment or condemnation. Later I realized it was just the opposite. He was using that space to do more than I could have hoped, beyond what my finite imagination could have dreamt. The treasures He wanted me to find along the way couldn't have been found elsewhere, and I couldn't have known the greatest prize—deep intimacy with Christ—any other way. I pray that today's study reframes how you view the desert times and the waiting. Though the details are sometimes fuzzy, God's promise to bless your obedience is always crystal clear.

SESSION SEVEN VIEWER GUIDE

THE UNLIKELY PATH OF HEALING

God doesn't always bring our healing in the way we expect....

2 Kings 5:1-8

• Naaman was part of enemy territory; had skin disease

• Aram was relying on another King for healing. "Am I God!?"

≫ what am I relying on for <u>my</u> healing???? ≪

   • 2 kings 5:9-13

   • Naaman has this grand expectation of what God "should" do to heal him.

   • We're always wanting someone else to do <u>our</u> healing.

2 kings 5: ~~thru~~ 14-15

Colossians 1:21-22

yet Elijah offered to have him come over and be healed by God!

GROUP DISCUSSION

What one thing from this video teaching really resonated with you? Why?

When have you missed God's physical, emotional, or spiritual healing? Was it because you didn't recognize it, or did you reject it because it wasn't what you wanted? Explain.

In your weakness, is your first instinct to run to God? Or do you trust in physical things (money, influence, people)? Explain.

How can you lean on your Christian community for support but make sure you're doing the work that God is asking you to do (for yourself)?

How does pride get in the way of our obedience to God, and at times, our healing?

How was Naaman going down to wash in the water seven times an act of faith? What act of faith do you need to take today to be healed?

Video sessions available for purchase or rent at LIFEWAY.COM/NOOTHERGODS

Paula's Tossed Salad (serves 4-6)

INGREDIENTS:

Dressing:	Salad:
1 cup vegetable oil	4-6 cups mixed greens
⅔ cup granulated sugar	¼ cup green onions, chopped
1 teaspoon black pepper	2 ounces feta cheese, crumbled
1 teaspoon salt	¼ cup carrots, julienned
1 clove garlic, minced	¼ cup pine nuts
1 tablespoon fresh lime juice	1 cucumber, peeled and finely chopped
	½ cup sweet corn kernels

DIRECTIONS

For the Dressing:
In a small bowl, whisk together all ingredients. Pour into jar or bottle for storage. Shake well, and refrigerate to blend flavors. Shake well before every use. Chill while you make the salad.

For the Salad:
In a large bowl, combine all ingredients. Add a small amount of Dressing, or more as desired, and toss to coat.

The proportions for this salad are up to you. I've given you some recommendations to get you started, but make it to your tastes and preferences.

The dressing makes the salad great. It tastes light and is easy to make! This dressing recipe makes more than you will need for the salad. But keep it in the fridge, and you can use the remainder later.

CHOSEN TO BEAR FRUIT

Growing up in the home of a pastor resulted in picking up certain Christian words that weren't exactly common speech. Backsliding, sanctification, justification, and fruit bearing were a normal part of my vocabulary. I remember giving a card to one of my teachers on the last day of school thanking her for a very fruitful year. This is so weird. Absolutely no one refers to a high school class in terms of fruitfulness. Except me. Totally me. I don't presume that the word *fruitful* has become any more mainstream since those days, but I still cherish the idea. To bear fruit is to bear life knowing that that new life will bear even more life—this is the exponential nature of fruit bearing. I can't think of anything more meaningful than living a life that bears fruit for God's kingdom.

When the Lord first exposed my idolatry—the people and things in which I'd placed far too much hope—all I could see in front of me were attachments and entanglements from which I needed to be free. My view was cluttered with the false gods that ruled me and needed to be dethroned. My grandest hope at the time was to clear the space in my heart so I could make room for the one true God. This was a worthy but shortsighted goal. I was so overwhelmed by everything that needed to be cleared out that I forgot (or maybe I didn't really know) that God wanted more than my heart tilled up and neatly weeded. He wanted to move in and plant something new. In other words, I was clearing the land without considering what would happen if God actually planted new seeds in that soil and those seeds blossomed with fruit. I just hadn't thought that far ahead.

In John 15, after having gathered His disciples together, and just before He went to the cross, Jesus spoke to them about bearing fruit. He wanted them to know that He'd chosen and appointed them to make an impact for His kingdom. Their lives were to have eternal purpose. Their fruit-bearing would look different than merely achieving goals, gaining wealth, or building enterprises. The fruit of their ministry would be seeing the dead come to life in Jesus, the lame tossing their mats aside, and wayward souls turning from idolatry to the living God. They would see men, women, and children giving their lives to Christ and the church growing with excitement and passion. I simply hadn't considered this promise and blessing of abundant fruit when writing *No Other Gods* the first time around.

Some of this fruit has been the surprise of my life. When out of obedience I parted with what I considered essential relationships, I was amazed at how the Lord eventually replaced those relationships with kindred spirits who love me, but who more importantly love Jesus. When my career in music crumbled and touring the country abruptly ended, I couldn't have imagined the Lord sending me to places such as the Amazon and Moldova. When I let go of my own fame and renown, I had

no idea how infinitely more gratifying it would be to bear fruit for Jesus' fame and renown.

Dear friend, I don't presume to know what the master Gardener wants to cultivate in the space you're obediently and sacrificially clearing for Him. All I know is that whatever He has in mind, abundant fruit is part of His plan for you. And the fruit He bears in our lives is beyond compare next to the artificial highs of our false gods. It's like comparing an apple orchard in autumn to the bowl of wax fruit that used to sit on my grandmother's dining room table, they're fundamentally different.

I can't wait for you to get started on this last week of study. The hard work you've been doing will prove more worth it than you've ever dreamed. The Jesus you're pursuing is more worthy than anyone or anything you've set your heart on. He's chosen you and appointed you to bear fruit. Fruit that will last.

YOU'VE BEEN CHOSEN

JOHN 15:16a: You did not choose me, but I chose you.
I appointed you to go and produce fruit and
that your fruit should remain ...

When I first wrote *No Other Gods*, I was at the tail end of an intense season of sifting. The Lord had pruned some cherished parts of my life, and I had no idea what He would grow in the stead of those freshly cut places of loss. I simply clung to the hope that in the removing He'd cultivate something new. This was no small task of faith. It required separation from dear people I loved. It meant letting go in my heart of my dream career and struggling to support myself financially. All these years later I can tell you two things: The Lord is faithful, and He provides. He's filled those empty spaces with more than I could have hoped for, yet He's filled them very differently than I'd imagined.

During the initial writing of this study, I focused on the idea of dealing with our idols so we could make room for Christ. All these years later I've caught a glimpse of what He wants to do with that room—He wants to use it to bear fruit in our lives. There's a biblical premise I want to focus on in our last week of study together. You can squeeze a few things out of an idol: temporary pleasures, comfort, money, status, or a fleeting identity. But you'll never get supernatural, life-producing fruit. Only God, His Son, and the Holy Spirit can produce that kind of eternal meaning in our lives.

Jesus testifies to this in John 15:16.

Read John 15:16 below and fill in the blanks from your own version.
"You did not choose me, but I _____ you.
I _____ you to go and produce fruit and that your fruit
should remain ..."

The word *chose* is pretty straightforward. It means *to be picked out, elected.* What compares to the pure joy of being chosen out of a group for your skills or contributions? What in life rivals someone seeing you for your unique personality or qualities? This is what's so precious about marriage: one man and one woman choosing one another out of all others on earth to spend the rest of their days together.

In addition to being chosen, Jesus tells His disciples that they're also appointed. The word *appointed* means to set or put in a new position, to bring about a new arrangement. This is like being chosen within your chosen-ness. Like a football player who's already been chosen for the team but is now being appointed as quarterback. Or someone chosen for the choir who's being appointed for the solo. It's another layer of chosen-ness.

Now that we've considered being chosen and appointed, envision Jesus, the Son of God, staring into the eyes of His disciples mere days before His crucifixion. He's about to leave them, though not as orphans—the Holy Spirit will come in His place. Out of all the things He could have said to them in this moment, He says, *I've chosen you, I've appointed you*. This calling by itself is too much to fully fathom, but He continues by explaining what He's chosen and appointed them for.

What did Jesus call them to do?

Dear believer, it bears repeating that no idol can choose you for something like this, nor can it accomplish this kind of miracle in your life. The fruit we're chosen to bear is an eternal, supernatural kind that's borne out in the here and now. The next few days of study are going to be absolutely inspiring for those who long for their lives to matter for Christ's kingdom. My prayer is that during our final week together you'll catch a vision of the fruit you'll bear as a result of dethroning your modern-day idols.

To fully comprehend John 15:16, we need go back to the Old Testament and follow the thread of fruit-bearing in Genesis. I think you'll enjoy this journey. On days Four and Five of this week we'll return to John 15 and conclude our study together around the feet of Jesus.

READ GENESIS 1:11.

If you mainly get your produce from the grocery store (most of America) rather than from your own garden, it's easy to take fruits and vegetables and the seeds they carry for granted. But what is significant about fruit that carries seed of its own kind? Put another way, what does seed make possible?

NOW READ GENESIS 1:27-28.

What would be the result of God's blessing upon man and woman?

What was the first part of His series of commands?

Over the next few days we're going to record six points regarding fruit bearing. We'll list them on page 191 for quick reference.

At the very top of Genesis we see the first point:

1. It was God's intent from the beginning that we bear fruit.

Write this in the space provided on page 191.

PERSONAL TAKE: So far in Genesis we have seen two types of fruit: fruit as produce and fruit as children or descendants. Look back at John 15:16. What third type of fruit do you think Jesus is speaking of?

The Bible speaks of three types of fruit: 1. Fruit we eat, such as apples, oranges, and so forth; 2. The fruit of the womb, such as children and grandchildren; 3. Spiritual fruit, such as the fruit of the Spirit, making disciples, leading people to the saving knowledge of Jesus, and advancing God's kingdom here on earth. Today we'll focus on the fruit of the womb (Gen. 1). Understanding this type of fruit will give deeper meaning to the spiritual fruit the Lord has chosen each one of us to bear. (Note that the fruit of children and grandchildren can also be categorized as spiritual fruit.)

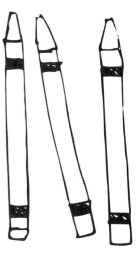

MOVE FORWARD TO GENESIS 6:5-7.

Why does it appear God's blessing of physical fruit bearing will come to an end?

READ GENESIS 6:8-10,22.

What is said about Noah in these verses that appears to keep the hope of physical fruit bearing alive? List every positive revelation about Noah's faithfulness to God.

After Noah obeyed the Lord by building the ark and then dwelling in it with his family during the flood, the Lord appeared to him with a significant blessing.

READ GENESIS 9:1.

What was the Lord's blessing on Noah and his sons, and how was it similar to God's blessing on Adam and Eve?

I encourage you to take time to read about Noah's journey between the point where God nearly wiped out humankind to the moment of God blessing him to bear fruit (Gen. 6–8). In the meantime, note point number two and write it on page 191:

2. Fruit bearing will always find a way in the soil of obedience.

Could it be that in your job, home, and church, the Lord is looking for you—out of everyone else—to walk purely before Him, to be obedient to what He's said, even if it seems outlandish at the moment? Explain.

Up to this point in Genesis, God's blessing of fruit bearing (childbearing) continued to move forward despite human wickedness. Approximately four hundred years after Noah, God called Abraham—one of Noah's descendants—out of his homeland and to a place the Lord would show him.

READ GENESIS 17:1-6,15-18.

What tension existed between God's promise to Abraham that he'd bear fruit (physical descendants) and his actual circumstances?

PERSONAL REFLECTION: In what area are you currently experiencing this tension between the fruit you know God has called you to bear and your current obstacles or impasses?

I spoke about this tension in greater detail in the Session Six teaching video because the Lord used this passage to change the direction of my life. All Abraham could see at that moment was what he knew—Ishmael. And Abraham wanted God to bless the very same person—Ishmael. I remember the Holy Spirit saying to me, *Kelly, do you trust me for the blessing you can't see, for what's not familiar, for what you can't now imagine?*

Abraham and Sarah grew impatient with God's plan and their actions produced the fruit of Ishmael. But God wanted to produce His fruit in them, which required a miracle. The result was Isaac. This brings us to the third point. Add the following to the list on page 191:

3. God's fruit can only be borne God's way.

PERSONAL REFLECTION: What of God's fruit have you become impatient for? What fruit of your own are you settling for?

The fruit God longs to bring about in your life is something only He can do.

The fruit God longs to bring about in your life is something only He can do. There will be no mistaking it for fruit produced by your savviness, luck, or hard work.

We'll continue to follow this thread of fruit bearing through a couple more patriarchs in the Book of Genesis. For now, I want you to consider your response to the Lord in relation to what you've studied today.

PERSONAL RESPONSE: What in God's Word has spoken to you most deeply today and why? What will you do in response?

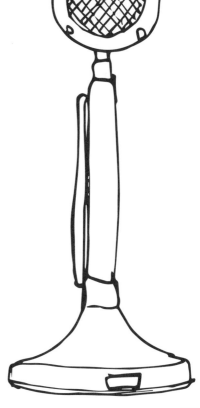

DAY TWO
GOD'S PERFECT TIMING

ECCLESIASTES 3:11: He has made everything
beautiful in its time (NIV).

I recently returned from a trip to Moldova, a small country situated in the southeast region of Eastern Europe. This was my fourth year in a row working in a rural village with Justice & Mercy International at our annual Children's Bible Camp. Each year our team enjoys building on the fruit of previous years.

The first year in this village the boys settled arguments by shoving each other to the ground. We were constantly consoling the little ones who'd wander over crying because the older ones had called them names or hit them in the gut. A few of the older kids would mock us to our faces because that's all that had been modeled for them. The little ones were painfully distrusting and standoffish. While all these behaviors were to be expected due to the conditions in which many of these kids live, we wondered how we'd ever make a dent in this survivalist culture often defined by poverty, alcoholism, and abuse. The thought of having to come back year after year seemed overwhelming, especially if our initial efforts proved ineffective.

But during this fourth year trip, every person on our team had noticed a striking improvement. Kids who were once skeptical of us jumped into our arms. A few of those who'd previously caused the most trouble asked if they could be junior leaders next year. Some who hadn't been ready for the gospel message were now eager to know Jesus. Moms who hadn't acknowledged us in the past were entering into conversations with us. What had begun as a camp of forty-five children had reached upwards of one hundred and fifty. We could see the visible results of a sustained effort.

This is a small example of how the fruit that God desires to bear in our lives is often produced over the long and sometimes difficult passage of time. He never forgets our labor of love.

READ GENESIS 24:1-37.

Abraham knew what it was to trust God for the fruit of descendants because he and Sarah had to trust God for Isaac. But by Genesis 24, Sarah had passed away, Abraham was well along in years, and Isaac was still unmarried. For Abraham to have the fruit God promised Him (all nations being blessed through him), he needed more than the miraculous birth of Isaac. He needed Isaac to marry and have children of his own.

What sign did Abraham's servant ask for from God (Gen. 24:12-14)?

I'm going to go out on a limb and guess you've never thrown out a fleece quite like this one (24:12-14). I'd love to be married, but I'm thinking the chances of my meeting a husband because I offered to water someone's camels are slim. Still, I've had a few profound experiences when the Lord did something specific in my life in unmistakable fashion.

READ GENESIS 24:50-61.

Take note of Laban's, Bethuel's, and Rebekah's reactions to what God was doing (vv. 50,58-60). Mark on the scale below how confident they seemed to be that God was at work in these circumstances.

1	*2*	*3*	*4*	*5*	*6*	*7*	*8*	*9*	*10*

Doubtful   *Positive*

PERSONAL REFLECTION: Briefly describe a time when the Lord spoke to you in a way you knew was unmistakably Him.

How does the blessing spoken over Rebekah in verse 60 keep with our theme of bearing fruit?

READ GENESIS 25:19-26.

How old was Isaac when he married Rebekah?

How old was Isaac when Rebekah had their twin sons?

PERSONAL TAKE: In light of the blessing pronounced on Rebekah in Genesis 24:60, how do you think these long years of barrenness might have affected Rebekah's faith in God? Take some time with this.

I can't help but think of the moment when Abraham's servant, Rebekah, and her family members gathered around the table considering and celebrating God's blessing on Rebekah. "This is from the LORD," they unanimously declared (24:50). They could see the divine markers. She would leave her familiar homeland and go on to lead a remarkable life in a foreign land. The next morning Rebekah mounted a camel's back and was carried off into the distance. A cloud of witnesses shouted a blessing over her. It went something like this, *Sister, sister! Thousands upon ten thousands will come from you. One day you'll own our enemies. Go let your life multiply more life. God's hand is all over you!*

The joy of a new marriage must have been blissful until it bled into the stark reality of her barrenness. She must have questioned God's blessing on her life in the growing years of a womb left empty. Was what God promised her a misunderstanding? Or worse, did she feel she had been misled? I wonder what she thought night after night in those exceedingly dark tents pitched under a desert's sky. Had she heard God wrong? Had everyone been mistaken? Was that whole camel-watering ordeal just a coincidence? Or was it providence? She most likely struggled with these questions for the twenty years between the promise and the beginning of its fulfillment.

PERSONAL REFLECTION: Has there been a time in your life when God made a promise, yet the fulfillment is still to come? Have you given up hope? Have you wondered if you heard Him right? (You may be thinking of the same situation you mentioned earlier today in the Personal Reflection.) Journal your thoughts below.

Genesis 25:24 in the CSB says, "When her time came to give birth …" "Her time" reminds me that while God doesn't always move *on* our timetable, His timing is a gracious gift *to* our timetable. On page 191, fill in point number four:

4. Fruit bearing is a process and processes take time.

Never have I tossed a seed into the ground, gone to bed, and woken up the next morning to a fully mature pepper, cucumber, or eggplant. I'm pretty sure I've had weeds grow this fast, but that's another story. The point is that fruit bearing requires time, and time requires faith, patience, and persistence. As the writer of Ecclesiastes stated: "He has made everything beautiful in its time" (Eccl. 3:11, NIV).

Fruit bearing requires time, and time requires faith, patience, and persistence.

I don't know all that God has promised you or what He's called you to. What I do know is you are to bear fruit for His glory. A lot of it.

PERSONAL RESPONSE: How will you demonstrate to the Lord your willingness to actively follow Him in your season of waiting? How will you renew your belief in what He's promised?

CLOSING PRAYER: Even when God has promised you something, it may not look exactly like what you think it will when He fulfills that promise. Take some time and surrender to God any expectations, knowing that He is faithful and will give better than we can imagine.

I hope today has been encouraging for you. I don't want any of you to fall short of the fruit God wants to cultivate in your lives. I don't want you to miss the impact and meaning He wants you to have now and in generations to come. Wrestle it out with the Lord in your desert tent if you have to. Deepen your prayer life. Keep seeking. But whatever you do, don't stop believing Him. And don't return to your familiar idols. Your time will come.

DAY THREE
OUR FRUITFULNESS, HIS FAITHFULNESS

GENESIS 48:4a: He said to me, "I will make you fruitful and numerous."

So far we've looked at the thread of physical fruit bearing beginning with Adam and Eve, weaving its way through Noah and his family, Abraham and Sarah, and Rebekah and Isaac. We've seen how improbable God's promise to bring them descendants must have felt for many of these biblical characters at different times in their lives. Look back on page 191 at the four truths about fruit bearing you've recorded so far. Choose the one that's most meaningful to you, and write it in the margin of this page.

PERSONAL REFLECTION: Why is it the most meaningful?

Today we'll continue to walk through Genesis, recording two fruit-bearing truths that will be especially restorative to those who feel they've messed up too much for God to bear anything good in their lives. Quick question: Have you ever heard of Jacob? He'll challenge your inclination to think you're disqualified from bearing fruit because of an imperfect past. I promise today's study on his life will encourage you deeply. Not because Jacob is enough, but because our God is.

READ GENESIS 25:27-34.

What was Jacob's sin in this story?

READ GENESIS 27:1-40.

What were his sins in this instance?

Jacob would ultimately have to flee for his life from Esau. Jacob left for his uncle Laban's house, leaving his homeland behind. In the Session Five teaching video I talked about the part of Jacob's life where he married two wives, Rachel and Leah. Contention and unrest continued to follow him. He got in disputes with his uncle, was never what his wives wanted him to be, and finally ended up in a wrestling match with the Lord Himself. While I appreciate Jacob for many reasons, squeaky clean he is not.

LET'S PICK UP IN GENESIS 35. READ VERSES 1-14.

Who commanded the people to get rid of their foreign gods?
(Circle the correct answer).

                    God   *Jacob*

PERSONAL TAKE: God told Jacob to build an altar to the Lord in Canaan. Why do you think this command led Jacob to tell his family to get rid of their false gods?

We learned in our first week of study how easy it is to deceive ourselves into thinking we can worship God while clinging to our false gods. At this point in Jacob's life he knew that if he and his family were going to build an altar to the Lord they would have to do it with clean hearts and hands. They couldn't take their idolatry with them.

> *According to verse 4, where did Jacob hide (or bury) the false gods and earrings? (The earrings possibly had markings on them indicative of foreign worship and also could have been melted down into an object of worship.)*

It's interesting to note that the Canaanites would often worship under trees, which were symbols of abundant procreation. It's as if burying the false gods under a representation of the world's way of bearing fruit was a way for Jacob and his family to close the door on that old, false way of life. This freed them to turn to the one true God and what only He only could bring them.

> *Who receives the blessing of fruit bearing in verses 11-12?*

PERSONAL TAKE: Do you think Jacob deserved this covenant blessing from the Lord? Why or why not?

This brings us to the next point for you to fill in on page 191:

5. God's fruit in our lives does not depend on a past of perfect choices.

Write this one down slowly. Let its truth permeate your heart. If God's grace is overflowing enough to bless Jacob with peoples and nations, then He's able to take our imperfect pasts and redeem them for a future of fruit. Fruit that will last.

I want to close with one more passage from Genesis as we thread God's promise to bear fruit through His people's lives, even when we fall wildly short of the mark.

READ GENESIS 48:1-4.

Picture Jacob at the end of his life. He'd been a deceiver, a thief, a wrestler. He'd toiled between two wives, eventually burying Rachel along the road to Bethlehem. His sons had sold their brother Joseph into slavery, and he grieved his loss for many years thinking Joseph to be dead. He immigrated to Egypt in his old age. He'd even declared his years to have been "few and hard"—not exactly a chipper sentiment (Gen. 47:9).

And yet here in the final few hours of his life, Jacob—out of all the memories he could have returned to—goes back to the fruit God promised to bring about in his life.

READ GENESIS 35:11 AND 48:4 BELOW (EMPHASIS MINE).

God also said to him, "I am God Almighty. *Be fruitful and multiply.* A nation, indeed an assembly of nations, will come from you, and kings will descend from you."

GENESIS 35:11

He said to me, "*I will make you fruitful* and numerous; I will make many nations come from you, and I will give this land as a permanent possession to your future descendants."

GENESIS 48:4

What's the significant difference between God telling Jacob to "be" fruitful and God "making" Him fruitful?

PERSONAL REFLECTION: Why do you think Jacob recounts God's words to him in this slightly different way?

When God tells us to go "be" something, I wonder if He simply waits for us to take that step of obedience so He can then "make" so whatever it is He's called us to accomplish. I also wonder if Jacob looked back and realized that the fruit he'd borne and would continue to bear even after he was gone was only by God's grace, that only God could make him fruitful. This brings us to our last point from Genesis on fruit bearing (add it to the last slot of your list on page 191):

6. Our fruitfulness is based on God's faithfulness.

Yes, Jacob wrestled with God. Yes, he built altars to the Lord. Yes, he experienced a vision of angels ascending and descending in his dream. Yes, he led his family to purify themselves and get rid of the false gods at Shechem. And yes, Jacob was obedient at the end of his life to bless the younger grandson. But in the end, after all was said and done, Jacob knew he couldn't boast in his own achievements or blessings. For God had made him fruitful.

I hope this journey through Genesis has helped shape your understanding of the abundant, fruitful life the Lord intends for us to have—at least from an Old Testament perspective. I can't wait for tomorrow when we'll spring ahead to John 15 and learn more about fruit bearing in New Testament times, straight from the mouth of Christ.

THE ART OF REMAINING

JOHN 15:4a: Remain in me, and I in you.

As God's timing would have it, I'm writing the final two days of this study after back-to-back trips to Moldova and the Amazon. Eastern Europe and Brazil boast profoundly different cultures as you might imagine. For instance, the teenagers in Moldova tell me it's weird when I smile and wave at people while walking down the street. "Kelly, you're embarrassing us," they tell me while jabbing me in the side. "Strangers are suspicious if you're too friendly to them." Meanwhile, in Brazil, the women I meet squeeze me into their matronly bosoms, kiss me on both cheeks, and then start offering me food.

God wants your life to bear fruit wherever you are.

Experiencing different cultures never fails to enrich and broaden my thinking. But what I love most is seeing the gospel bear fruit all over the world—in cultures so different from one another and so vastly different from my own. You may not find yourself traveling to different countries, but be certain, God wants your life to bear fruit wherever you are—in your home, neighborhood, church, and in your workplace. God wants your life to bear fruit through the lives of your children and grandchildren, your nieces and nephews, and in your marriage. He wants you to bear fruit through your dearest friendships, acquaintances, and business relationships. He wants your life to be fruitful in your children's schools, where you go to college, and through your social media interactions.

Dear sister, your life is meant to matter. You've been chosen and appointed for impact. Your idols can't do this for you. Only in following Jesus will you discover the joy of a life that counts for something far beyond itself. For the remaining two days of our study, we'll be turning our attention to fruit bearing from the New Testament perspective. Make sure you don't miss the last video teaching session. It will cover important material from our passage today.

READ JOHN 15:1-17.

The metaphor that Jesus uses in this passage represents three people. Draw a line to make the appropriate connections below:

The true Vine	*Jesus*
The Branches	*God the Father*
The Vinedresser (Gardener, Husbandmen)	*Us*

Write down John 15:16 from your Bible in the space below:

Today I want us to look at how we get to this place of producing lasting fruit. In the teaching video session, I'll talk about being attached to Jesus as the true Vine and address the loving pruning of the Father. But in this lesson I want us to dwell on the word *dwell*—did you catch that snazzy pun?

Jesus uses the word *dwell* (*remain, abide*) eleven times in these seventeen verses. The Greek word is *menō* and means *to dwell, remain, stay, abide (i.e., lodge) with; wait for, continue, to exist.* I focused on this word in a study I wrote on 1, 2, and 3 John, *What Love Is*, because it's a word John often used. John also highlighted Jesus' use of the same word in his Gospel. It's significant to our study of *No Other Gods* because in this world we're continually tempted to find our refuge in a slew of lesser loves, pleasures, and comforts. Remaining in Christ will be our year-after-year, day-by-day, minute-by-minute safeguard, keeping us from turning back to our past idols. It will guarantee a life of meaning and impact for the glory of God.

REREAD JOHN 15:4-5.

PERSONAL TAKE: Jesus told His disciples that without Him they could do nothing. What do you think Jesus meant, in light of knowing people who don't abide in Christ yet accomplish lots of things, many of them good? (Look at both verses carefully.)

Jesus says we're to remain in Him and He in us. He mentions both sides of this coin a few times in this passage, indicating that both sides are significant. Write the distinctions below:

Jesus remaining in you:

You remaining in Jesus:

If I haven't stated this enough, my desire for this study is to see you abandon your false gods. But if you stopped there, that would only be half the battle and ultimately a losing one. What we want in the place of our idols is the intimacy that comes through abiding in Christ and the eternal fruit that bursts forth as a result of that abiding.

Let's look at three ways we can actively remain in Christ.

PERSONAL REFLECTION: Turn to the back of your Bibles and read 1 John 3:24. (We'll be flipping back and forth between John and 1 John and 2 John, so be careful to note the references.) What is it about personal obedience to Jesus' commands that keeps you in a constant state of abiding in Him?

Return to John and read 15:9-10. According to this passage, fill in the blank below.

We remain in Jesus' love when we obey His _____. (Find the numbered list at the end of today's study and write this sentence down next to #1.)

READ JOHN 15:12-13.

How does Jesus want us to love others?

TURN TO THE BACK OF YOUR BIBLE AGAIN, AND READ 1 JOHN 3:16-18.

We see in this passage that withholding compassion and resources from those in need stands in opposition to the love of Christ remaining in our hearts. John goes on to further explain that we can't just say we love people, we must show them through our actions and by sharing His truth.

We can't just say we love people, we must show them through our actions and by sharing His truth.

Why do you think it's contradictory for the love of Christ to remain in a person while he/she withholds compassion from those in need?

NOW READ 1 JOHN 4:9-12.

PERSONAL REFLECTION: Both of these passages employ the word *menō* (remain/reside/abide/dwell in your translations). At first glance, you may assume you've got "loving others" covered. But may I ask you, are you withholding from someone in need? Are you loving in both action and truth? Are you loving like Jesus loved you? Are you loving by laying down your preferences, desires, even your rights? Know that I am asking myself these same questions, just as desperate for Christ to transform my heart. Record your answers.

We remain in Jesus when we _____ others. (Write this sentence down next to #2 in the numbered list at the end of today's study.)

We'll close today by looking at a third way we can be assured we're abiding in Christ.

READ JOHN 15:7.

What's vital to a productive prayer life?

I can't overstate how essential Jesus' words are to us. Our current culture uses a riptide of words contrary to Christ's teaching, dragging us away if we're not filled with His truth. And the messages that sound almost like Jesus can be even more damaging because they are harder to identify. Ask yourself, "Are the messages I'm hearing lacking the truth or love of Jesus?"

READ 2 JOHN 7-9.

PERSONAL TAKE: What do you think it means to go beyond Christ's teaching?

We remain in Jesus when we remain in His _____ . (Finish the numbered list at the end of today's study by writing this sentence down next to #3.)

I hope today has been both convicting and encouraging. The only way our idols will grow strangely dim is through a day-by-day abiding in Jesus. And the only way we'll bear fruit that will last is through that same abiding. Today you recorded three truths that will help you remain: obeying Christ, loving others, and knowing His words. Tomorrow we'll look at the benefits that accompany a life that remains in Christ. I can't wait to share this last day of study with you.

WE REMAIN IN JESUS AND THEREFORE BEAR FRUIT, WHEN:

1.

2.

3.

DAY FIVE
THE BENEFITS
OF ABIDING

JOHN 15:15b: I have called you friends ...

Well here we are. At the end of what I pray has been a life-changing journey for you. What began with Pharaoh and the Israelites is ending with Christ and His bride, the church. Where we once lived for idols that have no power to satisfy, we've cast our gaze and set our affection on Jesus in whom we remain and who remains in us. In the places of pruning and loss, we're beginning to experience a life of significance and meaning, our lives a branch budding with fruit. Where we once chased after our false gods, we're now learning to abide in the true Vine.

As we conclude our study together, I want to leave you with the benefits of a life firmly attached to Jesus.

READ JOHN 15:9-17 AGAIN SLOWLY.

According to verse 11, what single word sums up why Jesus spoke this teaching? Write the word and circle it.

Perhaps when Jesus mentioned "these things" in verse 11, He wasn't only referring to the words He'd spoken in John 15 but all the words He'd shared with His disciples. This is why I hope in the days ahead you will continue to immerse yourself in God's Word because through His Word we have joy.

PERSONAL REFLECTION: What words of Jesus have brought you joy during this study? Cite one or two specific examples.

READ VERSES 12-13 AGAIN.

What single word describes how Jesus commands us to relate to others? Write the word and circle it.

One of the greatest benefits of abiding in the true Vine is a supernatural ability to love others, even to the point of laying our lives down for them. This is not the kind of love the world offers, a love based on feelings, deservedness, romance, or conditions. Instead, the love that seeps from the sap of the true Vine, and into the branches of our lives, shows mercy when it's not merited, grace that can't be explained, kindness when it's not deserved, and compassion for the forgotten. Your idols will never love you this way, nor produce this kind of love in you.

PERSONAL RESPONSE: How can you show the love of Christ to someone you may have written off?

READ JOHN 15:14-15.

Instead of "servants," what does Jesus now call His disciples?

Jesus uses the Greek word *philos* to describe those who love Him and obey His commands as an expression of that love. It means *friend, beloved, loved.*

In the columns below, describe the difference between a slave and a friend, according to verses 14-15.

SERVANTS/SLAVES	FRIENDS

PERSONAL REFLECTION: What idols have you been enslaved to? In what ways have those false gods proven that they're not a friend to you? (This may seem like a funny question, especially if your false god is an object or substance, but it may be telling.)

So far we've discovered the benefits of joy, love, and now we see the benefit of friendship, or intimacy with Christ. Write the word intimacy *in the space provided and circle it.*

If you've ever believed the lie that Jesus is not relational, that He's distant and doesn't speak, consider verse 15. Jesus tells us His business. He shares with us His heart. He directs our paths. He reveals the secret things out of His Word. We've talked a lot in our study about how easy it is to look to people to meet all our longings. We know by now that when we look to any one person to meet the deepest needs of our hearts, when we put intimacy with that person in the place of God, we miss out on friendship and communion with Christ.

A life in the Vine is a life in which you are never alone.

As a single woman I'm blessed with a tremendous community. I have dear friends who know me deeply. I'm close with my family and am part of a loving church. But nothing ultimately satisfies me like hearing the words of Christ spoken to my heart in accordance with His Word. I don't write this as pie-in-the-sky fodder. I know loneliness, I know fear, and at times I've known depression. I know what it's like to go to bed at night, every night, without anyone beside me. But I also know the intimacy of Christ, and He has more than supplied my needs and many of my desires. A life in the Vine is a life in which you are never alone.

READ JOHN 15:16-17.

You should already know by now that one of the benefits of abiding in the true Vine is that you'll bear fruit that will last. Write the word fruit *below, and circle it.*

According to verse 16, what can we expect the Lord to do for us when we're abiding in the Vine? He will _____ our prayers. (Circle this sentence.)

I love what the late Andrew Murray wrote about this passage, "Beloved disciple, seek above everything to be a [person] of prayer. Here is the highest exercise of your privilege as a branch of the Vine."[1] Remember that this verse isn't a license to claim whatever we want in the name of Jesus, nor is it a guarantee that God will give us whatever we pray for. Think of the context here. It's all about bearing fruit. It's seeing people set free from the bondage of their sin, reaching out to the poor and unpopular, discipling believers, loving our children, serving in our church communities, laying our lives down in our marriages and friendships. When we pray along these lines, I believe God will respond in unimaginable and unmistakable ways.

PERSONAL RESPONSE: When you consider bearing fruit for Christ, what is your single most important prayer going forward? Write it below, remembering that you're exercising your highest privilege as a branch of the Vine.

Though not an exhaustive list, today you've written and circled five benefits of abiding in Christ: joy, love, intimacy, fruit, answered prayer. As we close our study, we'll add one more benefit, perhaps the most important and glorious of all.

LOOK BACK AT JOHN 15:1-3.

According to verse 3, what did Jesus say the disciples already were?

This verse seems to come out of nowhere. It's the one verse that doesn't appear to fit. Where does the word *clean* come from, and why does Jesus insert it right in the middle of a speech about abiding in the vine, being pruned, and producing fruit? This becomes clear when we look at the Greek words for *prune* and *clean*. They're almost identical. Both mean *pure, clean, spotless*.

Follow me here: Jesus tells His disciples that God the Father will be their Vinedresser (husbandman, gardener) by pruning them, which is also a way of cleaning them. This is a picture of sanctification, that daily cleansing of our sin that ultimately transforms us more and more into the image of Christ. Still, verse 3 talks about a cleaning that's more thorough, more final, something that's already happened as a result of Jesus' words concerning Himself and salvation. I believe He was talking to His disciples about the forgiveness of sin that would come through His sacrifice alone.

The disciples were clean because of the salvation they had in Christ. This is a picture of justification, where Jesus declares us perfectly pure before God the Father, not because our good works have outweighed our bad, not because we're inherently decent, and not because God's turned a blind eye to our past, but because Jesus who knew no sin became sin for us so that we might become the righteousness of God (2 Cor. 5:21).

PERSONAL RESPONSE: If you've gone through this whole study and have yet to come into relationship with Jesus Christ, I would have no greater joy than to lead you in this prayer of repentance and faith:

> Dear Jesus, I recognize that I am a sinner in need of a Savior. I realize that I'm powerless to scrub myself clean of my sin. I believe that only You can fully cleanse my heart, transforming me and making me new. I believe this forgiveness is only possible because of Your death and resurrection on my behalf.

If you prayed this prayer I believe with deep joy that the words of Jesus are for you: You are clean. If you prayed this prayer, turn to page 199 for next steps.

> But now he has reconciled you by his physical body through his death, to present you holy, faultless, and blameless before him.

COLOSSIANS 1:22

The ultimate cleansing of our hearts needed not a gardener's shears but a sacrificial Lamb. I praise God that He will continue to prune us where we need it, but I praise Him more that He sent His Son Jesus to cleanse us to our core, once and for all. No other god can do this.

SIX POINTS OF FRUIT BEARING:

1.

2.

3.

4.

5.

6.

SESSION EIGHT VIEWER GUIDE

BEARING FRUIT

John 15:16
What's the purpose of ridding selves of idols?
- So we can be free to serve & love God.
- and to BEAR FRUIT 🍎 (enduring fruit!)
- We were <u>appointed</u>! ♡ (quality fruit)

Bearing fruit vs achieving goals ??
John 15:1-8 HOW TO BEAR FRUIT?

- God = pruner
- Jesus = vine
- Us = branch >> Vine + Branch = FRUIT

GOD....
- Prunes BAD for GOO
- Prunes GOOD for BETTER!

we bear fruit when we're attached to the true vine!!

Heb 12:11

With idols, we don't want any pruning — we become fearful of the PRUNER.
- God also prunes branches that bear fruit to bear <u>more</u> fruit.

GROUP DISCUSSION

Vine + Branch + Pruning = MORE FRUIT

*can also be really painful.

What one thing from this video teaching really resonated with you? Why?

Why are we more often impressed by the appearance of fruit than the quality of it? How does social media play into this?

What's the difference between achieving goals and bearing fruit?

As you've cleared out the idols of your heart and made room for God to dwell and act, what fruit are you seeing from your life or do you anticipate growing?

When have you experienced the pruning of God? Was it difficult to see God's kindness in His pruning? Explain.

How are you doing at remaining in Christ? What hinders you the most from doing so?

Don't fear be he is the one who makes us beautiful !!!

We serr a GOD father...

* We bear <u>more</u> fruit when we're surrendered to the vinedresser and don't be fearful of what he has planned — you will glorify GOD in the process.

Greek Orzo Pasta with Chicken (serves 6)

INGREDIENTS:

Pasta:	1 cup kalamata olives, halved or chopped
1 (12-ounce) package of orzo pasta	2 tablespoons fresh parsley, sage, and oregano (optional)
2 red, yellow, or orange bell peppers, diced	6 grilled, baked, or sautéed chicken breasts
½ medium red onion, diced	
1 medium cucumber, chopped	Dressing:
3 plum tomatoes, chopped or	½ cup olive oil
8 ounces cherry tomatoes, halved	2 lemons, juiced
3 garlic cloves, minced	2 garlic cloves, minced or pressed
8 ounces feta cheese, crumbled	Salt and black pepper, to taste

DIRECTIONS

Cook orzo pasta according to package directions, drain, and set aside in large bowl. Add bell peppers, red onion, cucumber, tomatoes, garlic, feta, olives, and fresh herbs. In a separate bowl, whisk together all Dressing ingredients. Pour Dressing over pasta, and toss thoroughly. Place chicken breasts atop pasta, and serve.

I've fallen in love with this recipe because it's fresh, easy, healthy, and feeds a lot of people at once. Plus, it's easily adaptable for different tastes. For instance, my brother has yet to be enlightened and still hates olives, so I can leave them out or put them on the side. You can also substitute other seasonal vegetables for the cucumber. Have fun with this one.

How do we get "much fruit"??

└→ "Remain in me, and I in you"

Vine + Branch + Pruning + Remaining = MUCH FRUIT

were in this for the long haul!

Goal

make room for the one True God! So he can work & do things we can't even conceive of!! ♡

SESSION EIGHT: CHOSEN TO BEAR FRUIT

193

Leader Guide
INTRODUCTION

No Other Gods is a video and discussion based Bible study and part of The Living Room Series. The weekly personal study along with the teaching videos will promote honest conversation as you study Scripture together. Since conversation is essential to the experience, you'll find a few starter questions in both the Viewer Guides and Leader Guide to help get the discussion rolling.

The recipes were added in hopes that they encourage groups to eat together, because so many great friendships and conversations naturally begin around a dinner table. That said, this study may be used in a variety of large or small group settings including churches, homes, offices, coffee shops, or other desirable locations.

TIPS ON LEADING THIS BIBLE STUDY

PRAY: As you prepare to lead *No Other Gods,* remember that prayer is essential. Set aside time each week to pray for the women in your group. Listen to their needs and the struggles they're facing so you can bring them before the Lord. Though organizing and planning are important, protect your time of prayer before each gathering. Encourage your women to include prayer as part of their own daily spiritual discipline, as well.

GUIDE: Accept women where they are, but also set expectations that motivate commitment. Be consistent and trustworthy. Encourage women to follow through on the study, attend the group sessions, and engage with the homework. Listen carefully, responsibly guide discussion, and keep confidences shared within the group. Be honest and vulnerable by sharing what God is teaching you throughout the study. Most women will follow your lead and be more willing to share and participate when they see your transparency. Reach out to women of different ages,

backgrounds, and stages of life. This is sure to make your conversation and experience richer.

CONNECT: Stay engaged with the women in your group. Use social media, emails, or a quick note in the mail to connect with them and share prayer needs throughout the week. Let them know when you are praying specifically for them. Root everything in Scripture and encourage women in their relationship with Jesus.

CELEBRATE: At the end of the study, celebrate what God has done by having your group share what they've learned and how they've grown. Pray together about what further steps God may be asking you to take as a result of this study.

TIPS ON ORGANIZING THIS BIBLE STUDY

TALK TO YOUR PASTOR OR MINISTER OF EDUCATION OR DISCIPLESHIP: If you're leading this as part of a local church, ask for their input, prayers, and support.

SECURE YOUR LOCATION: Think about the number of women you can accommodate in the designated location. Reserve tables, chairs, or media equipment for the videos, music, and additional audio needs.

PROVIDE CHILDCARE: If you are targeting moms of young children and/or single moms, this is essential.

PROVIDE RESOURCES: Order leader kits and the needed number of Bible study books. You might get a few extra for last minute sign-ups.

PLAN AND PREPARE: Become familiar with the Bible study resource and leader helps available. Preview the video session and prepare the outline you will follow to lead the group meeting based on the leader helps available. Go to *lifeway. com/NoOtherGods* to find free extra leader and promotional resources for your study.

EVALUATE

At the end of each group session, ask: What went well? What could be improved? Did you see women's lives transformed? Did your group grow closer to Christ and to one another?

NEXT STEPS

Even after the study concludes, follow up and challenge women to stay involved through another Bible study, church opportunity, or anything that will continue their spiritual growth and friendships. Provide several options of ministry opportunities the members can participate in individually or as a group to apply what they have learned through this study.

SESSION ONE

1. Welcome women to the study, and distribute Bible study books.

2. Watch the Session One video.

3. Following the video, lead women through the Group Discussion section of the Session One Viewer Guide (p. 9).

4. Close the session with prayer.

SESSION TWO

1. Welcome the women to Session Two of *No Other Gods*. Use the following questions to review their previous week's personal study.

What truth from this week had the greatest impact on you? Why?

In your own words, what's the definition of a *false god*?

What does trying to worship both God and your idols look like in your life?

What currently holds power over you? Why do you allow this to happen?

Are you using your gifts for God's glory or for your own glory, pride, comfort, happiness, or selfish motive? Explain.

Why are our hearts and treasures so intimately connected?

2. Watch the Session Two video, encouraging the women to take notes as Kelly teaches.

3. Following the video, lead women through the Group Discussion section of the Session Two Viewer Guide (p. 36).

4. Close: Spend time together praying for God to set free those who are bound to their false gods, who've given power over their lives to their idols. Consider giving women the opportunity to outwardly admit this, then gather around and pray for each one specifically.

SESSION THREE

1. Welcome the women to Session Three of *No Other Gods*. Use the following questions to review their previous week's personal study.

What truth from this week had the greatest impact on you? Why?

Why do we too often try to find our identities in our false gods?

Describe a time when you were convinced you had to fix something on your own because God wasn't moving fast enough or in the way you hoped He would.

Why do you think God purposefully allows, and/or brings, pain into your life? Describe a time you experienced this personally and how it affected your faith in Him. How does knowing He's good help you through these times?

Why do we so quickly turn to a false god to help us when we feel as though God is silent?

Share a time that fear spiritually paralyzed you. Then follow that up by sharing how you moved from fear to faith in that situation.

2. Watch the Session Three video, encouraging the women to take notes as Kelly teaches.

3. Following the video, lead women through the Group Discussion section of the Session Three Viewer Guide (p. 59).

4. Close: Ask women to form groups of two to four people and share how fear is currently paralyzing them. Instruct them to pray for each other after the time of sharing.

SESSION FOUR

1. Welcome the women to Session Four of *No Other Gods*. Use the following questions to review their previous week's personal study.

What truth from this week had the greatest impact on you? Why?

What is *comparison thinking*? How have you allowed yourself to be discouraged, discontented, or trapped in this kind of thinking?

Kelly quotes Michael Wells in this session: "Often the enemy uses facts to add to and augment his position. He will use true things, but he never uses them to lead a person to truth." What does that mean? How have you experienced that in your life?

How does the enemy intimidate us with lies? Why might that drive us to false gods? Have you personally experienced this?

What's the danger of leaving the doors of our hearts and minds open to screens? Which unfiltered screen has the most damaging effect on you?

Are you currently dwelling or abiding in the Word of God? What is your biggest hindrance to spending time in Scripture? Why is it so important that we do so?

2. Watch the Session Four video, encouraging the women to take notes as Kelly teaches.

3. Following the video, lead women through the Group Discussion section of the Session Four Viewer Guide (p. 86).

4. Close: Remind women that knowing who Jesus truly is, is critical to knowing what's really true. And to know Him you have to spend time with Him in prayer and in His Word. Challenge your group to make time with Jesus a priority this week.

SESSION FIVE

1. Welcome the women to Session Five of *No Other Gods*. Use the following questions to review their previous week's personal study.

What truth from this week had the greatest impact on you? Why?

What have you learned this week from the story of Rachel and Leah?

How can the good desire of wanting to be loved become a detrimental one? Have you ever experienced such a season in your life? Explain.

Why do we continue to fall for the trap of thinking that if we can just get what we want, we'll be happy?

How do you see jealousy, manipulation, arrogance, strife, and so forth playing out on social media? How can you keep from sinking into this swirl?

What does it mean that God is jealous for us? How have you seen God display His divine jealousy for you?

2. Watch the Session Five video, encouraging the women to take notes as Kelly teaches.

3. Following the video, lead women through the Group Discussion section of the Session Five Viewer Guide (p. 112).

4. Close: Briefly review how easy it is to put a person on a pedestal and make that person into a false god. Encourage women to take some individual quiet time with the Lord to evaluate their relationships and offer up the ones where the friend or loved one has become an idol.

SESSION SIX

1. Welcome the women to Session Six of *No Other Gods*. Use the following questions to review their previous week's personal study.

What truth from this week had the greatest impact on you? Why?

How does God use scarcity in our lives to draw us to Himself? Has that happened to you? Explain.

Has the Lord ever given you something you kept demanding even though it wasn't a good thing? Why would He do that?

Why do we allow obstacles to keep us from following God's call in our lives? Has this ever been your experience? What obstacles currently stand in your way?

What things are you holding on to that you're struggling to part with? How are they keeping you from moving forward with Christ?

Do you believe the following statements from the study: "There is nothing we can lay down that God cannot provide something better in its place. There is nothing we can lay down that God cannot resurrect"? What's the evidence of your belief?

2. Watch the Session Six video, encouraging the women to take notes as Kelly teaches.

3. Following the video, lead women through the Group Discussion section of the Session Six Viewer Guide (p. 138).

4. Close: Lead women to pair up and discuss what steps, big or small, God is asking each one of them to take. Direct them to pray for each other to have boldness and courage to take those steps.

SESSION SEVEN

1. Welcome the women to Session Seven of *No Other Gods*. Use the following questions to review their previous week's personal study.

What truth from this week had the greatest impact on you? Why?

Have you ever experienced a season of spiritual starvation? Explain. How does the Lord want to meet your needs in those times?

Why is it so important that we remember what God has done for us in the past? How does that help us move forward?

Why is shame so devastating to our spiritual lives? How has God helped you overcome this debilitating emotion?

Are you able to trust God in all situations regardless of the outcome? Explain.

Why is endurance important in dealing with your false gods? How are you doing at persevering? Explain.

2. Watch the Session Seven video, encouraging the women to take notes as Kelly teaches.

3. Following the video, lead women through the Group Discussion section of the Session Seven Viewer Guide (p. 164).

4. Close: Direct women to share what is hindering their trust in the Lord. Lead in a prayer thanking God for being trustworthy and for being patient with us when we find it difficult to trust Him.

SESSION EIGHT

1. Welcome the women to Session Eight of *No Other Gods*. Use the following questions to review their previous week's personal study.

What truth from this week had the greatest impact on you? Why?

How have you seen God bear fruit through your life?

How does waiting on a promise of God to be fulfilled make us vulnerable to trusting a false god? When have you experienced this?

How can you show a willingness to actively follow God even in a season of waiting?

What does it mean to remain in Christ? Why is it so important that we do? How are you personally doing at remaining in Him?

When you consider bearing fruit for Christ, what is your single most important prayer going forward?

2. Watch the Session Eight video, encouraging the women to take notes as Kelly teaches.

3. Following the video, lead women through the Group Discussion section of the Session Eight Viewer Guide (p. 192).

4. Close: Spend time debriefing the study. Encourage women to share how the Lord has spoken to them, how God has changed them through the study, and what steps they still need to take to get rid of their false gods and create room for the one true God. Share your gratefulness for their participation, and pray a prayer of blessing over your group as you close.

Appendix

BECOMING A CHRISTIAN

Romans 10:17 says, "So faith comes from what is heard and what is heard comes through the message about Christ."

Maybe you've stumbled across new information in this study. Or maybe you've attended church all your life, but something you read struck you differently than ever before. If you have never accepted Christ but would like to, read on to discover how you can become a Christian.

Your heart tends to run from God and rebel against Him. The Bible calls this *sin*. Romans 3:23 says, "For all have sinned and fall short of the glory of God."

Yet God loves you and wants to save you from sin, to offer you a new life of hope. John 10:10b says, "I have come so that they may have life and have it in abundance."

To give you this gift of salvation, God made a way through His Son, Jesus Christ. Romans 5:8 says, "But God proves his own love for us in that while we were still sinners, Christ died for us."

You receive this gift by faith alone. Ephesians 2:8-9 says, "For you are saved by grace through faith, and this not from yourselves; it is God's gift—not from works, so that no one can boast."

Faith is a decision of your heart demonstrated by the actions of your life. Romans 10:9 says, "If you confess with your mouth, 'Jesus is Lord,' and believe in your heart that God raised him from the dead, you will be saved."

If you trust that Jesus died for your sins and want to receive new life through Him, pray a prayer similar to this to express your repentance and faith in Him:

"Dear God, I know I am a sinner. I believe Jesus died to forgive me of my sins. I accept Your offer of eternal life. Thank You for forgiving me of all my sin. Thank You for my new life. From this day forward, I will choose to follow You."

If you have trusted Jesus for salvation, please share your decision with your group leader or another Christian friend. If you are not already attending church, find one in which you can worship and grow in your faith. Following Christ's example, ask to be baptized as a public expression of your faith.

ENDNOTES

SESSION TWO

1. Kenneth Sande, *The Peacemaker* (Grand Rapids: Baker Books, 1991), 104.

2. Richard Keyes, as quoted by C. J. Mahaney, "The Idol Factory," *Sovereign Grace Ministries* (website), accessed July 20, 2017. http://trinity-at-the-marketplace.org/printfiles/idol_factory.pdf .

3. John Calvin, as quoted by C. J. Mahaney, "The Idol Factory," *Sovereign Grace Ministries* (website), accessed July 20, 2017. http://trinity-at-the-marketplace.org/printfiles/idol_factory.pdf .

4. Douglas K. Stuart, *The New American Commentary, Volume 2 - Exodus* (Nashville: B&H, 2006), mywsb.com.

SESSION THREE

1. *The Cosby Show*, "How Ugly Is He?" Season 1, Episode 9. Directed by Jay Sandrich. Written by John Markus. NBC, November, 1984.

2. A. W. Tozer, *The Pursuit of God* (Harrisburg, PA: Christian Publications, Inc., 1948), mywsb.com.

SESSION FOUR

1. "Wise," Blue Letter Bible, accessed August 16, 2017. https://www.blueletterbible.org/lang/lexicon/lexicon.cfm?Strongs=H7919&t=KJV.

2. Michael Wells, "Day 85: Facts!," *My Weakness for His Strength, Volume 1* (Littleton, CO: Abiding Life Press, 2011).

SESSION FIVE

1. "epithymeō," Blue Letter Bible, accessed August 16, 2017. https://www.blueletterbible.org/lang/lexicon/lexicon.cfm?Strongs=G1937&t=KJV.

2. Timothy J. Keller, "Christ Our Life," January 15, 1995, sermon, MP3 audio, 15:26, http://download.redeemer.com/sermons/Christ_Our_Life.mp3.

3. J. C. Ryle, *Holiness* (Chicago: The Moody Bible Institute of Chicago, 2010), 55.

SESSION SIX

1. Timothy J. Keller, "Real Faith and the Only Son—the Gospel According to Abraham," June 17, 2001, sermon, MP3 audio, 25:05-29:03, http://www.gospelinlife.com/real-faith-and-the-only-son-5241.

2. Ibid., 27:46.

3. Ibid.

4. Tozer, mywsb.com.

5. Ibid.

6. Ibid.

7. Ibid., Timothy J. Keller, "Real Faith and the Only Son—the Gospel According to Abraham," 41:45.

SESSION SEVEN

1. C. H. Spurgeon, "Sweet Stimulants for the Fainting Soul," *The Metropolitan Tabernacle Pulpit, Volume 48* (Pilgrim Publishing House, 1977), mywsb.com.

2. Gary V. Smith, *The New American Commentary, Volume 15b - Isaiah 40–66* (Nashville: B&H Publishing Group, 2009), mywsb.com.

3. Ibid.

4. Ibid.

5. Stephen R. Miller, *The New American Commentary, Volume 18 - Daniel* (Nashville: B&H Publishing Group, 1998), mywsb.com.

SESSION EIGHT

1. Andrew Murray, *The True Vine* (Chicago: Moody Publishers, 2007), mywsb.com.

NOTES

NOTES

NOTES

DIG DEEPER INTO THE BIBLE WITH ADDITIONAL STUDIES FROM KELLY MINTER.

ALL THINGS NEW
A Study on 2 Corinthians
8 sessions

Explore the anchoring truths of bearing treasures in jars of clay, meeting Christ through a pressing thorn, opening wide your heart in the midst of hurtful relationships, and what it means to embrace the lost and lonely as ministers of the new covenant.

Bible Study Book 006103969 **$12.99**
Leader Kit 006120661 **$69.99**

LifeWay.com/AllThingsNew

NEHEMIAH
A Heart That Can Break
7 sessions

Nehemiah's heart was so broken for those in need that he left the comfort of his Persian palace to help them. Are you ready to let God break your heart for a hurting, lost world and move you to be the hands and feet of Jesus?

Bible Study Book 005371581 **$12.99**
Leader Kit 005461775 **$69.99**

LifeWay.com/Nehemiah

WHAT LOVE IS
The Letters of 1, 2, 3 John
7 sessions

Delve into the Letters of 1, 2, and 3 John, written to encourage followers of Jesus to remain faithful to the truth. Glimpse not only the heart of John but also the heart of Jesus.

Bible Study Book 005635536 **$12.99**
Leader Kit 005635537 **$69.99**

LifeWay.com/WhatLoveIs

RUTH
Loss, Love & Legacy
6 sessions

If you've ever felt devastated, struggled as a stranger in an unfamiliar place, or longed to be loved, you'll find a loyal sister in Ruth. Her journey of unbearable loss, redeeming love, and divine legacy comes alive alongside a companion CD of original songs written and performed by Kelly.

Bible Study Book 005189427 **$12.99**
Music CD 005275025 **$12.99**

LifeWay.com/Ruth

LifeWay.com/KellyMinter
800.458.2772 I LifeWay Christian Stores

LifeWay | Women

Pricing and availability subject to change without notice.